Lynda Field is a trained counsellor and psychotherapist who specialises in personal and group development. She is the author of many best-selling titles, including *Weekend Life Coach*, *60 Ways to Feel Amazing* and *60 Ways to Change Your Life*. In addition to giving seminars and workshops worldwide, she runs a telephone and online coaching service, and writes articles for a variety of national magazines. She lives in Essex, UK.

Visit Lynda online at www.weekendlifecoach.com or email her at lyndafield@weekendlifecoach.com

Fast Track to Happiness

From Fed-up to Fabulous in 10 Days

Lynda Field

Vermilion
LONDON

3 5 7 9 10 8 6 4

Published in 2007 by Vermilion, an imprint of Ebury Publishing

Ebury Publishing is a Random House Group company

The Random House Group Limited Reg. No. 954009

Addresses for companies within the Random House Group
can be found at www.rbooks.co.uk

A CIP catalogue record for this book is
available from the British Library

Penguin Random House is committed to a sustainable future for
our business, our readers and our planet. This book is made from
Forest Stewardship Council® certified paper.

FSC	MIX
www.fsc.org	Paper from responsible sources FSC® C018179

Printed and bound in Great Britain by Clays Ltd, Elcograf S.p.A.

ISBN 9780091912932

Copies are available at special rates for bulk orders. Contact the sales
development team on 020 7840 8487 for more information.

To buy books by your favourite authors and register for offers, visit
www.rbooks.co.uk

Contents

Dedicated to You:
May you be full of happiness.

Acknowledgements

My heartfelt thanks to:

Richard, my husband – Adventurer
Leilah, my daughter – Healer
Jack, my son – Intrepid Explorer
Alex, my son – Writer
Alaska, my granddaughter – Actress
Barbara and Idwal Goronwy, my parents – Soul Mates
Sue Roberts – Queen of Kindness
Alison Weatherly – Queen of the Needles
Barbara Higham – Queen of Courage
Phraid Gower – Queen of Determination

All my clients, colleagues and readers who inspire me to keep writing.

The wonderful and happy team at Ebury who are always behind me. With extra special thanks to:

My editor Judith Kendra – tactful, clever and gracious.

Caroline Newbury – resourceful, upbeat and creative.

And we should consider every day lost on which we have not danced at least once. And we should call every truth false which was not accompanied by at least one laugh.

FRIEDRICH NIETZSCHE

Introduction
Yes, You *Can* Feel Fabulous!

Happiness: state of well-being characterised by emotions ranging from contentment to intense joy.

DICTIONARY DEFINITION

If you are reading this book because you have lost some of your zest and enthusiasm for life then I can show you how to put a spring into your step and a lightness into your heart so that you can meet the new day with optimism. And if you are feeling low and finding it hard for to imagine ever feeling upbeat and happy again, hang on in there and keep reading; a more positive mood is just around the corner!

Whatever your emotional state, just stop for a moment and take a measurement of your happiness level right now. What do you score on the fed-up to fabulous scale if the lowest you can go scores 1 and the most wonderful you can feel scores 10?

TOTALLY   FABULOUS
FED-UP

   1   2   3   4   5   6   7   8   9 10

Don't despair if you are struggling to raise a smile; I have designed *Fast Track to Happiness* with you in mind; you *can* feel fabulous! This book will help you raise your energy and your mood, whether you are feeling as flat as a pancake, bored and disinterested in life or just a bit off-centre and not at your best.

The desire for happiness is a great motivator; of course we all want to feel really wonderful. And if that isn't a good enough reason for us to increase our smiles per day then just take a look at the findings of new research by psychologists at the Universities of California, Missouri and Illinois.

Their study showed that happy individuals are greater achievers and more successful in their careers and in relationships than those with a more miserable attitude. The researchers found that this was because the happier people were, the more they were inclined to go for new goals and to welcome new challenges and experiences. Their positive moods also made them more outgoing, energetic and popular – characteristics that also helped them to do well. The results showed that the more cheerful people are likely to earn more, have happier marriages and also to live longer than their more miserable peers. These interesting findings contradict the widely held assumption that having money, a great partner or the right job necessarily leads to happiness. Dr Sonja Lyubomirsky, who led the study, said: 'Our review provides strong support that happiness, in many cases, leads to successful outcomes, rather than merely following from them.'

Perhaps you can think of a time when you were feeling very happy and optimistic. Just remember how 'alive' and energised you felt; yes, the world was your oyster and you couldn't put a foot wrong. When we are in the happiness zone we feel positive, hopeful, openhearted, forgiving, creative and in top form. Isn't it wonderful to feel like this?

And it seems this buoyant mood helps us to attract the very best outcomes into our lives. When clients talk to me about their goals, and I ask them why their success is so important to them, they usually say that it is because it will make them happy. But as we have seen, maybe we are looking at this the wrong way round; it seems that if we make happiness our goal then all the rest might just fall into place.

Happiness has become a hot topic in academic circles with great interest in the development of the new 'science of happiness', which brings together the very latest research in medicine, psychology and social science. In 1998 Professor Martin Seligman began a new psychological movement that focused on the life-enhancing power of positive emotions and thoughts. Seligman had been researching depression for thirty years when, to the surprise of the American Psychological Association, he announced that Psychology had gone off track. He said that, rather than focusing on negative states of mind in an effort to control depressed states, psychology should be focusing on increasing peoples' happiness by discovering and studying the secrets of a happy life. The new positive psychology (sometimes called the science of happiness) has shown that psychologists can demonstrate ways to increase our happiness levels rather than just trying to stop us from being depressed.

And so the results of the research into happiness demonstrate two conclusions that have great implications for all of us: that happiness can create success and that we *can* increase our own individual happiness levels. These findings confirm what many of us have experienced. When we are feeling good then we attract the most positive results and when we are low we just seem to be a magnet for even more negativity. We also know that some thoughts and activities can lift our mood whilst others just bring us down. But although we are aware of these things and might know only too well that some of our behaviour is not conducive to creating contentment or joy, we can sometimes still find it very hard to step out of our gloomy mood and into the happiness habit.

If we concentrate on our deficiencies and our perceived 'faults' we will obviously feel despondent and unable to effect any useful changes. The more we beat ourselves up the less likely we are to feel contented. Of course this is obvious and yet we still do this to ourselves. Some of you will know only too well how this negative downward spiral works:

feeling badly about self → unenthusiastic attitude → low expectations → ineffective behaviour → poor feedback from others → increasing levels of unhappiness

So when positive psychology advocates that we concentrate on our personal qualities and build on our strengths rather than obsessing over what we think we can't do, we recognise that this makes sense. And when it suggests that we take time to identify the sources of happiness in our lives and then seek to spend more time doing what makes us happy, we again know that this is obviously a good idea.

For nearly twenty-five years I have worked as a personal development consultant; training, counselling and coaching people who want to make their lives happier and more successful. I have worked with the famous and the not so famous; with businesses; charities; counselling services; the unemployed; schoolchildren; the bereaved and many, many others. Experience shows me that each and every one of us wants to be happy but we often just don't know where to start and how to continue.

I have written *Fast Track to Happiness* to provide you with a clear and effective plan to lift your mood and change the quality of your life. This book sets out the easy daily steps that you will need to follow in order to change a bleak outlook into a bright and positive one. The 10-Day Happiness Programme gives you all the information and guidelines that you will require to transform your mood from fed-up to fabulous. You *can* be happy and you can learn how to stay happy. You might not believe that this is possible and if you feel like this I would ask you to suspend your disbelief for ten days and just follow the programme. I promise you that this book can lift your mood, taking you out of gloom and despondency and straight into the happiness zone. You only need to commit yourself to putting your own happiness first for the next ten days; if your goal is to be happy then you have bought the right book.

The programme provides an integrated approach to creating and attracting happiness. This simply means that I have taken the very best ideas from many disciplines; some are at the cutting edge of scientific research and others are steeped in ancient tradition. Each day of the programme will introduce strategies and tips taken from such fields as positive psychology and cognitive behavioural therapy, as well as new techniques from up to the minute coaching and counselling theory.

How to use *Fast Track to Happiness*

If you read this book at your leisure, dipping in when you feel the need then you will certainly experience the benefit. Life is often very busy and all-consuming and any little reminder to slow down and focus on our happiness is sometimes all it takes to get us to smile again. But there are times when we need more than this to see us through.

To get the very best results from *Fast Track to Happiness* you need to follow the guidelines. Each of the ten days is carefully designed to introduce a special set of ideas and techniques that work on balancing every aspect of your being: your mind, body, spirit and emotions. A happy person feels balanced and calm, and each day of the programme seeks to create these feelings within you. Many of my clients have used this system and I have seen the amazing affect it has had on them. I know that it is absolutely possible to change from an Eeyore to a Tigger!

Change is easy when we are relaxed and calm and so you will find time and space to unwind with the Refresh and Renew sessions in every chapter; these will show you exactly how to chill out and tap into a wonderful feeling of inner tranquillity. Each day will include Tips and Activities that introduce quick and simple ideas that will lift your mood – instantly! Before you begin the 10-Day Happiness Programme you will need to buy a happiness journal. Go out and trawl the stationers for the most gorgeous spiral bound notebook you can find. Some people go to great lengths to decorate their journals and if you are feeling creative why not go for it? At the end of the ten days your journal will be full of fascinating bits of information about you. It will be full of surprises and reflections and maybe even photos, poems and mementos. Creativity is a key to balance and harmony so feel free to make the most beautiful happiness journal in the world!

THE 10-DAY
HAPPINESS
PROGRAMME

Day 1
Wake Up with a Smile

If in our daily lives we can smile, if we can be peaceful and happy, not only we, but everyone will profit from it.

THICH NHAT HANH

I like living. I have sometimes been wildly, despairingly, acutely miserable, racked with sorrow, but through it all I still know quite certainly that just to be alive is a grand thing.

A GATHA C HRISTIE

Happiness is what we want and we pursue countless pleasures in quest of this goal. But even on a happy day that fantastic feeling of wellbeing can have a transient quality. So how can we get happy and stay happy?

Life brings changes and surprises and some of these are welcome and some are not; s**t happens! as the saying goes. And even when it's not happening we can still feel unaccountably miserable. Whether you are feeling slightly less than your best or feeling totally fed-up there is a way for you to lift your spirits.

Because I write books about self-esteem and confidence others often assume that my life is a smooth journey and that I've got it 'cracked' in some way. At workshops and talks people often ask me what it's like to be upbeat all the time and I have to come clean and say that I'm not! I certainly go through peaks and troughs, my life is not always easy, but having spent twenty-five years studying, researching and working on self-development issues for myself, my clients and my readers, I *have* learned how to feel that 'just to be alive is a grand thing'! If we can feel glad to be alive *whatever is going on*, then we are definitely in a win-win situation because then nothing can take our happiness away.

Furthermore it seems that difficulty, hardship and challenges can actually be the making of us rather than the breaking of us. Psychologist Dr Nick Bayliss, an expert in the field of the science of happiness, takes an extremely encouraging and constructive approach to the management of life's difficulties and even makes this suggestion: 'Could it be that first-hand knowledge of misery can be our incentive to master happiness?' He is not suggesting that life has to be a struggle to be worthwhile, but he does say this: '. . . it seems that by facing and surmounting problems we can grow not only stronger, but happier, than if our journey had been uneventful. An appreciation of this open-ended relationship between initial circumstances and their eventual outcome forms the very bedrock of lives that flourish.'

Today we will be looking at how it can be possible for us to appreciate our life even when things are not looking so good. You might be thinking that if I only knew what you were going through I would never dare to make this suggestion. But imagine this: you begin your day with a smile and know that you have got what it takes to rise to anything that life throws at you. You immediately experience a flood of endorphins (feel good hormones which you produce when you smile), which makes you more confident and moves you into a positive and optimistic mood. Now did you imagine it? If you did then you will already be feeling the good effects and if you couldn't do it then start practising. Why delay the experience of happiness when you can feel it right now, in this very moment? Because we are so often inclined to look at a situation and see the potential negatives before the positives (our 'catastrophic brains' at work) we can easily miss out on the sheer pleasure of just being alive. England's rugby hero Jonny Wilkinson is aware of this tendency in himself and says: 'I want to learn to smile more. My enjoyment is always retrospective. I get caught up in the challenges and pressures. Later on, I think: Oh I suppose I enjoyed that.'

Change one thing at a time

Each day I will ask you to make changes about the ways that you think feel and behave. This technique is called Change One Thing and it is something that you will get used to doing as the days go by. Try the first one now.

CHANGE ONE THING

ABOUT THE WAY YOU BEGIN YOUR DAY

THINK ABOUT WHAT COULD MAKE IT EASIER TO GET GOING ON A POSITIVE NOTE WHEN YOU WAKE UP. THE MOOD YOU WAKE UP WITH CAN COLOUR YOUR EMOTIONS FOR THE WHOLE DAY SO IT IS VERY IMPORTANT TO START WELL. HERE ARE A FEW POSSIBILITIES TO CONSIDER.

- YOU MIGHT DECIDE TO HANG UP A NOTICE TO YOURSELF WITH A SMILEY FACE ON IT SO THAT YOU CAN RAISE A LAUGH AS SOON AS YOU SURFACE.

- OR MAYBE YOU WOULD BE HAPPY TO OPEN YOUR EYES IF YOU KNEW THAT THE NIGHT BEFORE YOU HAD LAID OUT YOUR CLOTHES IN READINESS FOR THE MORNING.
- PERHAPS YOUR AWAKENING WOULD BE EASIER IF YOU SET YOUR ALARM TEN MINUTES EARLIER SO THAT YOU COULD HAVE A MORE LEISURELY START.

THINK ABOUT THIS AND THEN CHOOSE JUST ONE THING THAT YOU KNOW WILL MAKE A DIFFERENCE AND THEN WRITE IT IN YOUR JOURNAL. BEGIN TAKING ACTION TOMORROW MORNING.

Faced with so much lifestyle advice from experts on the television, in newspapers and magazines and on the self-help shelves, we can become weighed down by all the good things we 'should' be doing to get our lives together and feel happier. But there is a backlash to this, and some clients tell me that although they know lots of techniques they could be trying to help them feel better about themselves, there are almost too many choices to be made so why bother with any of them?

Fast Track to Happiness is designed to simplify the steps you need to take to change your mood from fed-up to fabulous, quickly. Rather than feeling overwhelmed by all the changes you might think you need to make, why not take it one easy stage at a time? Stop looking at that staircase and just take the first step by simply changing one thing that will make a difference to you. Once you do this you will begin an amazing process. It is so easy to become locked into habits that bring our energy down rather than raise it up and often it only takes a small alteration in our behaviour to bring about a massive result. There is something quite wonderful about making a firm commitment to do something that you know will work for you in a positive way. You will discover this as soon as you activate your first change.

HAPPINESS TIP

BECOME POSITIVELY AWARE

Pick up some happy-making positive energy by trying the following:

- Be on the lookout for anything of a positive nature such as a person's smile as you walk along the street.
- Hear the care and concern in someone's voice in an overheard conversation.
- Listen for uplifting words; what effect do they have on you and others around you?
- Watch people's body language and look for those who walk tall with a spring in their step.
- Notice how some people can override a negative comment and ignore a potential put-down.

As you focus on the positive energy around you, your mood will just lift higher and higher. Jot down any interesting conclusions in your journal.

If not now, then when?

Have you ever felt that your life is on hold and that you are just waiting for something or other before you can really get going and do what you want to do and be who you want to be? Clients often say that once they have done this or that they will then feel happy enough with themselves to go for what they want. We all know how easy it is to procrastinate but putting off our life until another day can never really be an option. This is it now; it's time to make an impact! Many years ago when I was umming and ahhing about which step to take next and why I wasn't ready to move on, my spiritual teacher said to me, 'If not now, then when?' This phrase has stuck with me and I ask it of you now.

Sarah's story

Sarah, 39, is a single mother who came for coaching because she was feeling 'stuck, unmotivated and depressed' (her words). Twenty years ago she was studying Fashion and Textiles at Saint Martins School of Art and Design and she loved it. Then she met Mark, a third year student, but after a few months she became pregnant and he said that he didn't want anything to do with her or the baby. Sarah left college and moved back with her parents who helped her with bringing up her daughter Jess. By the time Jess started school Sarah and she were living in a small rented cottage in a village in Sussex. Sarah had never stopped making beautiful cushions and bags and other one-off designer items and she soon began supplying a local craft shop. But whilst she loved what she did she had to sell to the shop at very low prices so she was always in dire financial straits. She said that she had struggled for years to manage and that lack of money was taking all the happiness out of her creativity. Local people had often asked Sarah's design advice for their homes but she had never felt confident enough to respond in a professional way so that she could actually make money from her expertise. By the time we met, Jess was just leaving home and Sarah was facing the prospect of living alone. When single parents become empty nesters they obviously face a huge change in lifestyle, which can be very daunting.

Over the years Sarah had done a number of courses in soft furnishing and upholstery work and she was well qualified to open her own business. But she had put it off for so long she said that it now seemed impossible to achieve. A week after Jess had left to start university Sarah decided that if she didn't act now her new business would never happen. We created a neat step-by-step action plan and after a few months she was already overwhelmed with customers. She is a new woman who loves her job and feels happy and satisfied by what she is doing. Sarah said to me that she didn't know why she had waited so long to fulfil her dream and that maybe the emptiness she felt when Jess left was the greatest incentive she could have had.

If you are feeling unhappy it might be because you are sitting on one (or several) of your dreams. Try the following activity to find out if you are.

ACTIVITY: I WILL DO IT WHEN . . .

THINK OF AN IMPORTANT GOAL. IT MIGHT BE A SECRET DESIRE OR IT COULD BE ONE THAT YOU ARE ALWAYS TALKING ABOUT. NOW WHY HAVEN'T YOU GONE FOR THIS GOAL? WHAT SORT OF EXCUSES DO YOU MAKE TO YOURSELF SO THAT YOU DON'T HAVE TO TAKE THAT FIRST STEP? ARE THESE EXCUSES RELEVANT? AND IF YOU ARE NOT GOING TO GO FOR THIS GOAL NOW, EXACTLY WHEN DO YOU PLAN TO GO FOR IT? IF THESE QUESTIONS ARE DIFFICULT TO ANSWER JUST TRY FINISHING THIS SENTENCE:

I WILL DO IT WHEN . . . .

WHAT ARE YOU WAITING FOR? START NOW TO MAKE YOUR DREAMS COME TRUE AND YOU WILL FEEL SO MUCH HAPPIER ABOUT YOURSELF.

What brings us happiness?

Clinical psychologist Dr Ellen Kenner hosts a radio show in America called *The Rational Basis of Happiness* where she has talked about the enigma of happiness. She says that 'There are many people who we think should be happy but are not' and that 'There are many people who we think should be miserable but are not . . . . Some people who seem to have nothing are very happy. Some people who seem to have everything are not. Yet some jet-setters seem happy while some moral crusaders have become miserable grouches.' Happiness can indeed seem very unpredictable, inconsistent and impossible to measure.

We know that money can't buy it, but on the other hand we have a sneaky suspicion that a hefty salary rise would definitely raise our spirits; well, Richard Branson always seems to have a smile on his face (in spite of all his cash!). We also like retail therapy because it gives us a great buzz but we also know deep down that a new lipstick, a new bag and even some very fancy La Perla undies can only bring us a temporary blast of the feelgood factor.

Would more money, sex, status and power do it for you? Do you think that if you had more of these things in your life that your happiness levels would increase? It has been suggested that our culture is fixated on how to get more of these four items. And yes, you will no doubt agree that these things certainly sound pretty attractive. However all the scientific research data points to a rather different conclusion.

In 2004, the New Economics Foundation published a 'well-being manifesto' for government and policy makers. The think tank stated that: '. . . despite unprecedented economic prosperity we do not necessarily feel better individually or as communities. For example, data shows that whilst economic output in the UK has nearly doubled in the last 30 years, happiness levels have remained flat.' The report shows that while genes and upbringing influence about 50 per cent of the variation in our personal happiness, our circumstances (income and environment) only affect about 10 per cent. After basic needs are met extra material wealth has little or no effect on life satisfaction or happiness. The remaining 40 per cent is accounted for by our outlook and activities: our relationships, friendships and jobs, our engagement in the community, and our involvement in sport and hobbies. These findings have great implications for us and for our future happiness because they mean we really can take control of our wellbeing by simply altering our outlook and behaviour: the ball is in our court; we only need to make the right moves.

As you might imagine, the Dalai Lama's recipe for happiness does not include a trip to the shops and makes absolutely no mention of sex, status or power. He says that: 'The purpose of our life needs to be positive . . . . For our life to be of value, I think we must develop basic good human qualities - warmth, kindness, compassion. Then our life becomes meaningful, and more peaceful - happier.' As we contemplate these words of wisdom we can begin to see happiness in a slightly different way. Yes, we are part of the material world and of course we can enjoy the goods on offer but we need to remember that happiness is an inner state; we can never find it outside ourselves in any shape or form. Your happiness is a feeling within you; it is a state of mind and is a response to what is happening around you. The great news is that you can learn to feel this response whenever you wish, just by changing your way of thinking and acting with more positive awareness.

The cycle of happiness

When we are feeling low, anxious, worried or defeated it can seem as though we might stay in this pessimistic and downbeat place forever. Even though we know how quickly things change and how ephemeral our moods can be, the negative downward spiral of unhappiness can interfere with our logic and overwhelm us with its heavy black clouds.

The emotional distress that causes us to feel badly about ourselves leads to a negative outlook with low expectations (of self, others and life). This in turn affects our behaviour, which becomes hesitant and unsure. Others pick up on our ineffectiveness and self-doubt and withdraw their goodwill, which of course just leads on to increase our unhappiness. The big question is: how can we break this cycle?

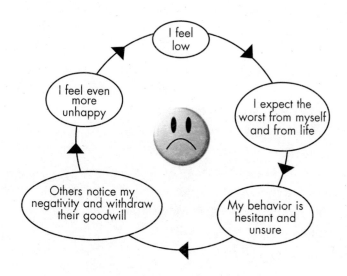

THE CYCLE OF UNHAPPINESS

Helen Keller is one of my favourite heroines and someone who always has a positive take on things. Although deaf and blind from infancy she was not the sort of woman who would ever let anything stand in her way. Whenever I find myself doubting my abilities to go for something I want (yes, I do this sometimes), I think of what Helen overcame and it helps me to get my lack of self-belief in perspective. She became an inspiring advocate for millions of people worldwide as she campaigned for peace, civil rights and the vote for women. This is one of my favourite quotes from her: 'When one door closes, another opens; but often we look so long at the closed door that we do not see the one which has been opened for us.' What a beautiful and symbolic image this is, but it is also of great practical use as it shows us how it is possible to move out from the cycle of unhappiness and into the cycle of happiness.

How does this help you? Are you sitting looking miserably at a closed door? If so, can you describe what this feels like? Imagine a new and beautiful door in front of you. Hold that picture and we will come back to it in a moment.

Now let us consider what it feels like when we are in the happiness zone. We feel upbeat and expect the best from our life, from ourselves and from others. This attitude leads to clear thinking, good decision-making and confident behaviour. Other people are naturally attracted to our positive energy and show their support for us and our ideas; all of which makes us feel even happier of course!

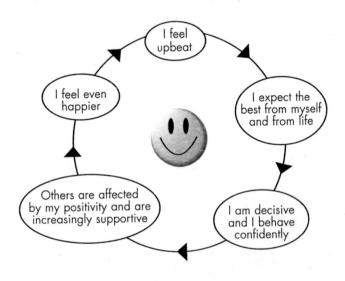

I feel upbeat

I feel even happier

I expect the best from myself and from life

Others are affected by my positivity and are increasingly supportive

I am decisive and I behave confidently

THE CYCLE OF HAPPINESS

Which cycle are you experiencing at the moment? If you are feeling energetically stuck behind a closed door why not bring to mind that beautiful new door that you have just visualised? Close your eyes if it makes it easier for you and just see your door in all its details. Is it made of beautifully carved wood? Is it metallic and heavy like the door of a safe? Or maybe it has a stained glass panel down its centre. Take the first image that comes to you. Now, with this picture in your mind I'm going to ask you to change just one thing about the way you are looking at the world.

CHANGE ONE THING

ABOUT YOUR PRESENT PERSPECTIVE

IF YOU WANT TO CHANGE THE WAY THAT YOU ARE FEELING JUST CONCENTRATE ON THE NEW DOOR THAT YOU HAVE VISUALISED. BEHIND THIS DOOR LIES A BRAND NEW PATHWAY FOR YOU.

- WHENEVER YOU FEEL READY, JUST IMAGINE YOURSELF WALKING UP TO THIS DOOR AND GRASPING THE HANDLE FIRMLY.
- TURN IT, AND AS YOU PUSH YOUR DOOR WIDE OPEN YOU SEE A SHINING PATH AHEAD OF YOU.
- WATCH YOURSELF TAKE THE FIRST STEP ALONG THIS PATH AND KNOW THAT YOU HAVE OPENED THE DOOR OF YOUR MIND TO A NEW POSITIVE EXPERIENCE.

WHEN YOU DO THIS VISUALISATION YOU ARE, IN EFFECT, TELLING YOUR SUBCONSCIOUS MIND THAT YOU ARE READY TO MOVE AWAY FROM YOUR OLD OUTLOOK AND ARE PREPARED TO STEP INTO SOMETHING BRIGHT, NEW AND DIFFERENT. BE IN NO DOUBT THAT YOUR SUBCONSCIOUS WILL REWARD YOUR ENTERPRISING GESTURE.

How wanting to be liked can affect our happiness

Of course we all want to be liked, it's part of human nature to seek the approval and consensus of others. But have you noticed how sometimes even though you have done your very best you just seem to face critical comments from the very people you were trying to please? Perhaps you can remember when this last happened to you and how you reacted. A client recently said to me that she wished that she didn't have such thin skin so that she could shrug off negative comments with a smile. Once we had begun to concentrate on her own levels of self-belief she found that she didn't care so much about what people thought of her as long as she felt good about herself. The key to happy and confident relationships is to stop taking everything so personally.

Criticism can hurt us terribly and cause us deep unhappiness but we can learn ways to control this emotional reaction. Happy people don't accept the blame for everything that goes wrong but neither do they expect themselves to be perfect. It is most unfortunate that one of the main symptoms of unhappiness is the feeling of deep self-criticism: we find it hard to love and appreciate ourselves when we are down. In fact, we become our own worst critics and this of course leads to a further depression of our spirits.

Next time you are feeling judged and found wanting by another person don't just go to that unhappy place where you want to shrivel up and disappear. Instead, start to become aware of your own individual reactions to the criticism of others. Consider this: if you believed that you didn't deserve a particular criticism then you would be able to laugh it off, wouldn't you? It would be just like water pouring off a duck's back.

Don Miguel Ruiz's book, *The Four Agreements*, was a huge bestseller in America a few years ago. In his book Don Miguel talks about our over-willingness to take everything personally which he says is a result of our being conditioned to fit into what our society deems to be 'acceptable'. He calls this conditioning process 'domestication' and says that it leaves us wanting to be liked by everyone and striving to be clever, stylish and sexy so that we can please all the people in our lives. This intense desire to be and do the right thing to keep everyone happy fills us with self-doubt as we measure our self-worth in terms of whether others are pleased with us, or not. Try the following quick quiz to see if your desire to please others might be standing in the way of your happiness.

Quick quiz: are you trying to keep everyone happy?

Look at the following statements, choosing answers A or B.

1 A friend has asked you a favour (the third one this week) and you just wish she would stop assuming that you will be at her beck and call.

A You agree to do it.

B You tell her that you are sorry but you just haven't time.

2 It feels like there are not enough hours in the day and you are stretched beyond your limit because you have taken on too much.

A You just try to do everything twice as fast and wind yourself up.

B You recognise the danger signs and let go of the least important items on your to-do list.

3 Someone you work with is very negative and her constant complaining gets you down.

A You always let her have her say even though you don't want to listen to her.

B You reply in a lighthearted way and outweigh her negativity with your positivity.

4 Someone makes an unjustified critical comment about you and you feel hurt.

A You feel like a fool and don't know what to say.

B You challenge the person and tell them that you don't deserve that sort of remark.

5 A family member is abusing your goodwill and you are fed-up.

A You feel too uncomfortable to speak up and so it carries on.

B You find a diplomatic way of making your feelings clear; you know that there is no need to fall out over this.

6 You are feeling justifiably angry.

A You don't want anyone to see your anger and you squash it as soon as you can.

B You are able to let yourself feel angry when it is necessary.

7 An acquaintance invites you to a party but you really don't want to go.

A You go anyway because you don't want to hurt anyone's feelings.

B You say that you would have loved to go but unfortunately you are busy that night.

8 You were tempted to buy a fabulous new dress in your lunch hour but you are worrying about what your partner will say.

A When you get home you hide it in the back of the wardrobe.

B You put it on and show him how wonderful you look.

9 The new boss at work seems to expect you to stay late most nights.

A You don't complain and just stay until she says it's time to go.

B You explain that you don't mind staying on occasionally but that most nights you need to leave on time.

10 Relatives are coming to your place for a big family get-together but on the day you feel ill and not up to entertaining.

A You just get on with it, you don't like to let everyone down.

B You know that they will all understand so you ring around and set a new date for the party.

11 You book a restaurant table for a special event and when you get there you find yourselves hidden away in a dark corner.

A   You say nothing and make the best of it.

B   You ask to be moved.

12 Everyone is leaving the domestic chores for you to do when you get home from work.

A   You get on with them because there's no point in asking for help, it's more trouble than it's worth.

B   You decide to get to grips with this once and for all and you make a rota which clearly allocates specific jobs to each member of the family.

13 Your boyfriend turns up late again.

A   If you say anything he will get angry so you don't challenge him.

B   You tell him that you don't feel that he respects your time when he keeps being late.

14 You have to make a very tricky decision and it's hard to know what to do for the best.

A   Other people keep giving advice and you just get more and more confused.

B   You listen to the opinions of others but in the end you do what your instinct tells you to do.

15 A friend keeps ringing you with her relationship problems and she talks to you for a long time most nights.

A   When she rings you always ditch your own plans for the evening because you want to be a good friend.

B   Next time she rings you tell her that you are on your way out but that you would be happy to talk next time you are free.

Score 1 for each time you answered A. Score 2 for each time you answered B.

If you scored 15–19

Your desire to keep others happy stands in the way of your own happiness. There are many occasions when you ignore your own feelings so that you don't have to rock the boat. Beneath your compliant exterior you probably feel very angry and unappreciated but you find it so difficult to put yourself first. Maybe you are afraid of how others will react if you begin to recognise and express your own needs.

Do this:

- Consider your own worth and recognise that your happiness is as important as anyone else's. If you give away your power to other people they will soon begin to treat you like a doormat.
- Don't teach others to treat you badly or you will always be unhappy and dissatisfied.
- Choose one instance where you need to be more assertive. Decide who you need to speak to and what you need to say and then just go and do it.

If you scored 20–24

Sometimes you do come forward and speak your mind, even if you know that it will displease others, but afterwards you often feel guilty and wish you had kept quiet. You hate being criticised and it is this that frequently prompts your desire to please everyone. Part of you is quite ready and able to act in your own best interests and you do know that you would be much happier if you were more resolute.

Do this:

- Say what you have to say and do what you have to do and respect yourself. Let go of those guilty feelings and trust your own judgement.
- The more you practise saying 'no' the easier it will get. Go out there and start practising.
- Cultivate your strong and assertive side; it will always guide you in the right direction.

If you scored 25–30

Well done! You know how to assert yourself and you are not a people pleaser. You have a healthy respect for yourself and the value of your time and so others are inclined to treat you well. Because your happiness levels are not dependent on what other people think you are much more in control of your own moods. You understand that although you will feel sad and low sometimes this isn't the end of the world and your mood will improve. Happiness is a state of mind and you are always ready to do what it takes to bounce back with a smile.

Do this:

- Keep working on your positive thinking, it is a wonderful strength that you can always fall back on.
- Take your fabulous happy vibes out into the world and share them; happiness is contagious.
- Find some new happiness habits in this book and add them to your repertoire and you will feel even happier!

Of course this issue of other people's happiness is not always clear-cut because sometimes another person's wellbeing *is* our happiness. For example, when do we stop being a kind and caring parent who is working for her child's good and become a downtrodden, taken for granted mum? And isn't it right to put our partner's wishes before our own sometimes; surely that is part of being in a loving relationship? If a family member or close friend needs our help and support we might need to put our own immediate wishes on the back burner.

There is certainly a thin line between being a good friend /partner/daughter/mother . . . and being a victim. Only you can know when you have crossed this line in any of your relationships. Some clues can be found in the way that you feel. If you are feeling angry, lacking in confidence, unappreciated, irritated, taken for granted, demoralised or any other similarly negative emotion you can be sure that you *have* crossed that line and that your happiness is being sacrificed for someone else's. If you recognise that this is happening in your life right now then take heart, you can change this situation. Begin to put your own wellbeing at the forefront of your life and remember that you can only give to others when you have something to give. The biggest gift you can share with anyone is the joy of happiness. Let your happiness come first for the next ten days and you will be renewed and regenerated. Your perspective will become much more positive and you will know exactly how much you are prepared to give to others and when to pull back and give to yourself. Increase your happiness levels and every aspect of your life will change for the better.

Now let's turn our attention away from thinking and analysing the concept of happiness. One of the most basic and obvious conclusions of all the research is that to feel happy we just need to do more of what makes us happy. And one thing that makes all of us happy is the ability to switch off and relax. Each day there will be a new relaxation technique for you to enjoy, so read the following instructions and then set the book aside for a moment as you put your feet up and take a moment to refresh and renew yourself.

REFRESH AND RENEW

A POCKETFUL OF SMILES

LAUGHING MAKES US FEEL GOOD BUT RESEARCH SHOWS THAT NOWADAYS WE ONLY SPEND SIX MINUTES A DAY LAUGHING COMPARED WITH EIGHTEEN MINUTES IN THE 1950s. SO WHY DON'T YOU JUST SIT BACK IN YOUR CHAIR, CLOSE YOUR EYES AND RELAX.

- NOW BRING TO MIND AN AMUSING INCIDENT, OR A GOOD JOKE THAT YOU HAVE JUST HEARD, OR ANYTHING THAT HAS MADE YOU LAUGH.

- AS YOU BEGIN TO REMEMBER YOUR LAUGHTER YOU WILL FEEL A SMILE CREEPING UP ON YOU.

- LET YOUR SMILE SHINE AND AS YOU DO YOU WILL NOTICE THAT YOU WILL FEEL UPLIFTED AND HAPPY.

- SIT WITH THESE SMILEY FEELINGS FOR A WHILE.

- AND WHEN YOU OPEN YOUR EYES KEEP YOUR SMILE ON AND SHARE IT WITH OTHERS.

THIS SOUNDS SO SIMPLE BUT IT IS ONE OF THE MOST EFFECTIVE WAYS OF SHARING HAPPINESS WITH OTHERS. WHEN I WAS A LITTLE GIRL AND LOOKING A BIT DOWN MY

> GRANDDAD USED TO SAY TO ME, 'LYNDA, HAVE YOU GOT A SMILE IN YOUR POCKET?' THIS ALWAYS USED TO MAKE ME LAUGH AND IT STILL DOES. SO WHATEVER IS GOING ON IN YOUR LIFE REMEMBER YOU HAVE A POCKETFUL OF SMILES TO HELP YOU ON YOUR WAY. JUST TAKE ONE OUT NOW AND SEE WHAT IT DOES FOR YOU.

Day 1 TODAY'S HAPPINESS ROUNDUP

At the end of each day, I will ask you take a few minutes to summarise your thoughts and feelings about the day and also to reflect on the main points that have been covered. This will be a great chance for you to review your own progress and also to notice which of the techniques have been most helpful to you. The main indicator each day will be how you score on the fed-up to fabulous scale which we first looked at in the introduction. The best way to do your daily happiness roundup is to start a new page of your journal and set out your page as follows. For this first day I have used a client's journal entry as an example.

MY HAPPINESS SCORE FOR THE DAY

TOTALLY   FABULOUS
FED-UP
  1   2   3   4 (5) 6   7   8   9 10

MOST SIGNIFICANT EVENT OF THE DAY

I found myself picking up all the cups in the office and cleaning the tearoom in my lunch break. Although I often do this I felt unusually cross today and so I stopped myself, left the mess and went out for a quick walk in the sunshine. When it was time to go home I noticed that someone else had finished cleaning up and I felt strangely elated!

MAIN CONCERN OF THE DAY

Because I am so aware of my happiness (and unhappiness) at the moment I realised that I spend a lot of time worrying about my partner's black moods. Whatever I am doing I often go back to thinking about how he is feeling and what I can do about it. I must usually do this unconsciously because today I just saw that he fills my thoughts at every spare moment.

WHAT CAN I DO ABOUT THIS, IF ANYTHING?

I did the *Are you trying to keep everyone happy* quiz today and I didn't get a very good score. This has made me consider how much I like to be liked and how sometimes this is so important to me that I think I have to solve everyone's problems for them. Logically I know I can't and so I am going to stop wasting all that energy on other people and use my time more positively, so that I feel happier in myself.

MOST USEFUL HAPPINESS STRATEGIES TODAY

Well, obviously the quiz opened my eyes. But the tip I loved most was the idea that you can spread happiness and take your smile out into the world and reach other people. I really got into it on my walk and I was amazed how ready people were to smile back. But I also noticed that it didn't go down so well with my partner. I think he sometimes controls the general mood at home by being quite gloomy most of the time. I hadn't really noticed this before either, so plenty to think about today.

WHAT WENT WELL TODAY

I managed to keep upbeat most of the time and I loved being a smiley person, I hadn't realised that I had got into a habit of not smiling. I had a great day because I was focusing on happiness strategies and I think that simply having this focus kept me tuned in to what was really going on. I like the idea of keeping my journal and I can't wait to try tomorrow's techniques.

THREE THINGS THAT MADE ME SMILE TODAY

When I opened my post at work and found an invitation to a colleague's wedding.

My dad phoned me to say he was feeling much better.

The newspaper seller called me a gorgeous girl!

When you have answered these questions you might like to add any other comments and interesting points that have arisen. You will be quite amazed by this journal when you read it after the ten days is over. I always encourage clients to use a notebook to record their personal thoughts and feelings and often when our sessions are over they decide to continue keeping a journal. Someone once told me that her journal had become like a wise best friend. She called it, 'A regular place to turn to whatever is going on.'

Now take a moment to consider the following reflections that summarise the main points of Day 1 and make a note of anything that has made a special impact on you today.

Final reflections

- Our life path takes us up and down and this is no bad thing for us because by facing and overcoming our problems we can grow stronger and happier.
- Genes and upbringing influence only about 50 per cent of the variation in our personal happiness and so we all have an opportunity and a choice to be happier.
- To increase our happiness levels we just need to do more of what makes us happy.
- We can never please all of the people all of the time and if we try to our own happiness will suffer.
- Smile and the world smiles with you.

Day 2
More Time for You

*The butterfly counts not months but moments,
and has time enough.*

RABINRANATH TAGORE

Lost, yesterday, somewhere between Sunrise and Sunset, two golden hours, each set with sixty diamond minutes. No reward is offered, for they are gone forever.

HORACE MANN

Ah yes, don't we know it's true; those precious 1,440 minutes per day are certainly whizzing by. But hey, who's got the time to stand around appreciating those sparkling time slots when there's just *so much to do and so few golden hours to do it in*? We might even be wondering if we have the time to be happy!

Journalist Carl Honoré came face to face with this dilemma when he found himself speed-reading his daughter's bedtime story. We have all had mad moments like this when we have suddenly stopped and realised that we had forgotten the real reason that we were doing something in the first place. Fast forward (actually make that slow forward!) to this evening when you: sit down to dinner; chat with friends; put your child to bed; make love . . . will you be enjoying every moment or will you be going through the motions of doing the task with your eye on the alarm clock? When Carl Honoré realised how his desperation to do more was taking him into the realms of the absurd he decided to fight back. The result was his internationally acclaimed book, *In Praise of Slow*, which has precipitated a worldwide movement that challenges the cult of speed. He describes being 'slow' as meaning 'living better in the hectic modern world by striking a balance between fast and slow'. No worries then about throwing out your computer and dishwasher and getting back to Stone Age basics.

Today we will be looking at ways to strike that magical balance between enjoying the amazing diversity of the material world and remembering to take pleasure in each and every precious moment of our lives. 'If only I just had more time'; how often do you say this? And what do you tell yourself that you would be doing with this extra stash of hours? I know you are busy and there are things that *must be done* before you can relax, but why not try a new approach? Instead of fighting the clock let's find a way to work with it. When you have a realistic and healthy approach to the concept of time you will find it possible to do more of all those wonderful things that make you happy. I can sense your resistance; perhaps you have read a few too many articles about time management; writing lists and prioritising. I know how you feel, and if you could see me now in my office with lists and research papers and notes cluttering every surface you would realise that I am on your side. I'm not knocking 'to-do lists' but I do know that it takes more than this to get our lives into a happy balance.

Hurried woman syndrome

Mahatma Gandhi once commented that, 'There is more to life than increasing its speed' and he was certainly on to something even then. I wonder what the great spiritual leader and political activist would have made of the rushaholic twenty-first century?

The Hurried Woman Syndrome (HWS) has been recognised as a new epidemic among British women and was first identified by Texan doctor, Brent Bost. In February 2005, the women's magazine *Prima* published the results of the first UK study of the condition. *Prima* questioned 10,000 women and discovered that more than 75 per cent of them showed signs of HWS. Now, are you wondering what the symptoms might be or do you know only too well what they are? You probably won't be surprised to hear that hurried women are overweight, tired and have a low sex drive!

Ruth Tierney, Features Editor of *Prima*, said: 'The results were shocking . . . Many of the women we interviewed instantly identified with the vicious circle of symptoms, which often begins with tiredness, leading to an increase in appetite, weight gain, and a loss of interest in sex and exercise. These changes kick-start a cycle of emotional symptoms including a lack of self-esteem, irritability, feelings of guilt and worthlessness, and a drop in motivation.' Ah, so perhaps now you know why you are not always at your fabulous best. But what's to be done?

Ms Tierney says, 'It seems the answer to this very modern condition is to go back to basics, and to stop trying to be the perfect wife, mother and employee.' And Dr Bost concluded that all us HWs should: 'Do the things granny would have told you to do. Basically, slow down and smell the roses, set priorities and realise you have limits.'

Before you shout in protest that you *haven't got the time* to smell a rose, or indeed anything else, let's get all this into perspective; you are not the only one who is in a hurry. Sociologists have now recognised the widespread effects of what they call 'time famine' which they suggest is due in part to our increasingly speed-driven methods of communication. Our mobile phones ensure that we are immediately contactable and that instant email whizzing through the ether often demands a similarly instant response. A Harvard Medical School doctor has even invented the term 'pseudo ADD' to describe the people who compulsively check their phones and emails every 30 seconds and so are unable to focus on whatever they are supposed to be doing.

On his website www.inpraiseofslow.com Carl Honoré, using the word 'slow' as shorthand for a new approach to time and space, talks about the concept of slow email. He says: 'These days, even technophiles are warming to the idea of speed limits on the information superhighway. A senior manager at IBM now appends this rallying cry to every email he sends: "Read your email just twice each day. Recapture your life's time and relearn to dream. Join the slow email movement!"' Mmm, you might be thinking your boss would not be too keen on this idea; but it's easy to relate to Carl's approach. Are you hooked on checking your phone and your email? Would you like to recapture some of your life's time? Start thinking about how you could begin to do this.

CHANGE ONE THING

ABOUT THE SPEED THAT YOU ARE THINKING AND MOVING

- SLOW DOWN NOW.
- AND IF YOU HAVEN'T GOT A ROSE TO SMELL FIND SOMETHING EQUALLY BEAUTIFUL TO ADMIRE.

- LET 'SMELLING THE ROSES' BECOME A METAPHOR FOR YOU SO THAT IF AND WHEN YOU FIND YOURSELF HURRYING TOWARDS FEVER PITCH YOU ONLY HAVE TO REMIND YOURSELF TO TAKE TIME OUT (OF ANY SORT) TO BREAK UP THAT INTENSELY RUSHED FEELING THAT CAN LEAD TO ALL THOSE HORRIBLE SYMPTOMS THAT YOU HAVE JUST READ ABOUT.

- WHENEVER YOU FEEL LIKE AN UNHAPPILY HURRIED WOMAN TODAY JUST REMIND YOURSELF OF THE PRICE YOU MIGHT BE PAYING FOR THE EXTRA SPEED YOU ARE GENERATING. AND SAY TO YOURSELF, 'STOP AND SMELL THE ROSES.'

THIS IS A GREAT HABIT TO DEVELOP BECAUSE IT REMINDS YOU TO TAP INTO YOUR OWN DEEP SENSE OF APPRECIATION AND WONDER. AND WHEN YOU MAKE TIME TO BE HAPPY YOUR FEELINGS OF GOODWILL WILL BENEFIT ALL THOSE AROUND YOU.

The way of the happy cat

This issue of slowing down our pace, taking time to stand and stare and living at a more natural and user-friendly rhythm might feel fraught with difficulties. This may be because we are thinking in extremes: we look at the hare and tortoise story and find that neither symbol is useful. The hare is a foolish speed freak that rests on his laurels a bit too long and is outsmarted by the ever-plodding tortoise. The moral of this story is lost on us. Slow but sure might win the race but only because the hare was a self-satisfied fool. Now out there in the world we can't afford to crawl at a snail's pace in the hope that all the fast hare-like people are equally daft; we have to find a way to take control of our lives but also to stay relaxed. This takes some doing, but there is a way.

By nature I am inclined to hare-like qualities; I actually love dashing about and doing things and feeling purposeful. But over the years I have been forced to recognise that this love of speed does come at a price. I have introduced all sorts of strategies to slow me down and although they work I always have to be vigilant about keeping myself balanced and out of overdrive. For example, I began yoga lessons for the obvious reasons and then found myself having to work faster in order to free up the time. Rushing to my office I shouted over my shoulder to my husband, 'I've got to get to work early or I'll never have time for the yoga class.' Richard raised one quizzical eyebrow and I had to laugh; point taken, he knows me well. Hare-like people can be addicted to rushing around so that they will find any reason to go fast, *because they like it!*

At the other end of the spectrum are those with slower and quieter tendencies. A tortoise-like person is more measured and deliberate but may have to bow out of the race because she just can't keep up. Tortoises have to get up to speed in order to survive but they are always looking for a chance to stop. If you are a hurried woman with tortoise tendencies you will find any reason in the world not to go fast, *because you don't like it!* Hares and tortoises often attract each other in relationships and help to give each other some balance.

But these aren't the only behavioural options. Between these two extremes is a middle way, the way of the happy cat. She is adaptable and flexible; can go fast when she needs to; knows when it's time to stop; loves stretching out and resting; is in touch with her sensual side and can hunt alone. I brought the cat into the story because she seems to epitomise the two qualities that we want to embrace: to be able to be stretched out languorously one minute and to be fast and focused the next. If the cat had been in Aesop's fable she would definitely have won the race and had time for a nap in the sun before the other two were even in sight of the finishing line. Try the following quick quiz to see if you are more of a hare, tortoise or cat.

Quick quiz: are you a hare a tortoise or a cat?

Read the following statements and ask yourself if they are true for you. Score as follows:

1   always
2   often
3   sometimes
4   rarely
5   never

1   I would describe myself as a busy person.
2   I expect the best of myself.
3   I am happy when I am on the go.
4   I am an organised hard worker.
5   I make lists, keep a diary and use a wall planner.
6   I multi-task whenever it is possible.
7   I feel unhappy taking a break when I know I still have things to do.
8   When I lose focus, I pull myself together and get going.
9   I need to be in control.
10   I like to achieve more than is expected of me.

If you scored 10–20

You have hare-like tendencies, but then you knew this already. You like rushing about and taking charge and sometimes forget that there is a downside to overactivity. The hare does eventually run herself to the ground and she may be addicted to adrenaline, so you need to slow up a bit if only for the sake of your health. Take some tips from the happy cat and indulge in some time outs. This might feel like torture at first but you will be happily surprised how this habit can grow. Start to schedule downtime into your diary and take your relaxation periods seriously. Although you might think that the faster you go the more you will achieve this isn't always the case. Inner balance is the key to happy and successful outcomes and you will want to feel good enough to celebrate your victories, won't you?

If you scored 21–30

You have hare-like inclinations but you are not a total speed freak. You do manage to give yourself a break occasionally but still sometimes go quite close to the edge. Reflect on the times when you are not pushing yourself too hard and notice how much better you feel then. Try to increase this feeling of wellbeing by finding other outlets for your incredible energy, such as running or going to the gym. Keep moving towards a more balanced approach. Remember how the happy cat takes many naps a day (and she has nine lives!).

If you scored 31–40

You are a happy cat in the making! If you scored at the lower end then you are an admirable example of a flexible and well-balanced person. You chase your goals but they don't dominate your life; you enjoy the journey as well as the outcome.

If you scored at the upper end you need to watch out for tortoise-like tendencies. You can be laid back but please don't fall asleep. Perhaps it would help you to get a bit more organised and focused. You need some direction in life if you want to feel happy and satisfied.

If you scored 41–50

Are you hibernating in your shell? Have you lost the confidence to get out there and take a slice of life? There is a huge difference between taking it easy and giving up. If you scored at the upper end then you need an injection of hare-like energy. Set some simple short term goals and take the first step to achieving them. Don't be afraid to take your role in life; you will feel unhappy and unfulfilled if you continually hang back watching others. Apply some structure to your day and you will really feel the benefit.

HAPPINESS TIP

HAVE MORE FUN

DR ROBERT HOLDEN, FOUNDER OF THE HAPPINESS PROJECT, SAYS THAT FUN, PLAY AND LAUGHTER ARE 'LIFE'S SHOCK ABSORBERS – WITHOUT THEM WE BECOME LESS RESILIENT AND LESS ABLE TO KEEP THINGS IN PERSPECTIVE'.

- MAKE A LIST OF TEN FUN AND FRIVOLOUS THINGS THAT YOU WOULD LIKE TO DO.
- DO ONE OF THEM.
- NOTICE HOW MUCH BETTER YOU FEEL.

OF COURSE IT IS JUST COMMON SENSE THAT WE WILL FEEL HAPPIER IF WE DO THINGS THAT MAKE US HAPPY. BUT SOMETIMES IT SEEMS THAT IT IS ALMOST TOO OBVIOUS. HOW OFTEN DO WE SIT AROUND POKING A STICK INTO OUR UNHAPPINESS AND STIRRING IT ABOUT SO THAT WE FEEL EVEN WORSE? IF YOU ARE GOING OVER AND OVER AN UNHAPPY INCIDENT THEN IT MIGHT BE TIME TO BREAK THIS NEGATIVE CYCLE AND HAVE SOME FUN!

If you are running on empty you will come to a standstill

You can't keep borrowing 'doing' time from the reserves that you need to set aside to just 'be'. The majority of us often do this and we may have become quite proud of our multi-tasking skills. But as we shift ourselves up a gear (yet again) so that we can be all things to all people, let's take a moment to review the situation; perhaps our super efficiency costs us too much both emotionally and physically. The report on the Hurried Woman Syndrome considers it to be a potentially dangerous condition, which 'can often be a precursor to clinical depression or serious illness'. If you are reading this and recognising your Super Woman self then you will certainly know that rushing and juggling and tearing about are taking their toll on your happiness in some way or another.

Jeanette's story

Jeanette, 43, is a primary school teacher married to Glen, 41, who is a doctor. They have three children aged 7, 10 and 12. When we spoke, Jeanette told me that Glen worked long hours in a big city hospital and that she has 'always picked up all the pieces on the home front'. Jeanette went back to work when her youngest was two because they needed the money and also she missed the independence that her career gave her. But things had reached crisis point for Jeanette by the time she came for coaching. She complained of being tired all the time and felt overworked and unappreciated. 'On a bad day I feel like a servant with so many demands and expectations laid on me. And I used to adore my job but now I am losing all my enthusiasm, maybe because I am so tired and fed-up. My days just seem to go on and on at a relentless pace and I wonder whether there will ever be any time for me. When I feel resentful like this I also feel guilty because I am so lucky to have a healthy and happy family and a good job. But I have lost myself somewhere and I need to find myself again.'

There was no question of Jeanette being able to give up work and Glen was stretched to full capacity at the hospital. There is no magic wand that solves Jeanette's dilemma (and that of many other women) but rather it is a question of taking specific steps to recreate some time and space to enjoy the simple pleasures of life. We looked at various lifestyle issues and I asked some questions:

How much exercise was she getting?

Who could she call on for childminding services?

What were her favourite leisure activities (when she last had leisure time)?

Was she eating well?

How was she sleeping?

It was no surprise to discover that Jeanette had very little exercise apart from being on her feet all the time at school. She said, 'We used to be in the Ramblers' Association before we had the children but I never get out for a walk now.' She ate on the run most of the time (multi-tasking as she did so) and she slept badly, waking up often, worrying about something that she had to do. But there was a light at the end of this tunnel because her in-laws lived nearby and were continually offering to have their grandchildren for the night so that Jeanette and Glen could get a break. When I asked Jeanette why she didn't take them up on their offer she said that she was always too tired to bother to organise it and anyway Glen wouldn't be interested. I suggested that she might talk to him about this and she did. She emailed me that night saying that she was 'blown out' by the conversation that she and Glen had just had. She said he was 'absolutely thrilled' about the prospect of time alone with her and had already been on the Internet to check out a weekend trip to Prague.

Jeanette was amazed to discover Glen was feeling as fed-up as her and was only too glad to discuss his feelings and what they might do to improve matters. Once they had opened up to each other things immediately began to look up. Jeanette said that as soon as she knew that she and Glen were working as a team again she felt her spirits rise. Over the next few weeks they managed to get away for a couple of weekends and it reminded them that their partnership was important and that they needed to give it some attention. She said, 'I still get tired of course but the magic has come back to our relationship. We take the children on long walks at the weekends and I love it, we take a picnic and make a real day of it. Anyway now I feel more balanced and I've joined a Pilates class and Glen and I have made a family rota for the domestic chores and everyone is making an effort to pitch in and help. It feels so much better to have said how I feel instead of just keeping this all to myself. I can't think why I carried on for so long without saying anything. Maybe women want to look like they can cope with everything but it's not fair to be expected to do everything, is it?'

ACTIVITY: MAKING MORE TIME FOR ME

IT *IS* POSSIBLE TO BREAK OUT OF A HURRYING CYCLE BUT IT NEEDS A CHANGE OF ATTITUDE AND RESPONSE FROM YOU. CONSIDER THIS: IF YOU CAN'T MAKE TIME FOR YOURSELF HOW CAN YOU EXPECT ANYONE ELSE TO MAKE TIME FOR YOU? YOU DESERVE TO TAKE THE TIME AND SPACE YOU NEED TO HAVE A HAPPY, BALANCED AND FULFILLED LIFE. TRY THE FOLLOWING:

- BE REALISTIC ABOUT TIME. IF YOU PRETEND TO YOURSELF THAT YOU CAN DO AN HOUR-LONG JOB IN THIRTY MINUTES THEN YOU ARE CREATING ENDLESS PRESSURE AND DISAPPOINTMENT FOR YOURSELF.
- EXPRESS YOUR 'HURRIED' WORRIES AND FEELINGS TO YOUR NEAREST AND DEAREST; PERHAPS THEY ARE UNAWARE OF YOUR PRECARIOUS JUGGLING ACT.
- DELEGATE! I KNOW, NO ONE CAN DO THE JOB LIKE YOU CAN BUT UNLESS YOU ARE HAPPY TO BE ON DUTY 24/7 YOU MUST BE PREPARED TO SHARE THE DUTIES (AT HOME, AT WORK, EVERYWHERE!).
- RELISH YOUR TIME ALONE DOING NOTHING OR DOING SOMETHING THAT YOU ABSOLUTELY LOVE TO DO. PRACTISE LOVING YOUR LIFE; THE MORE YOU DO THIS THE HAPPIER YOU WILL FEEL.
- TURN OFF THE PHONE AND STOP CHECKING EMAILS WHEN YOU ARE OFF DUTY (FOR EXAMPLE IN THE EVENING OR AT THE WEEKEND).
- TAKE UP A RELAXING ACTIVITY: AN ART CLASS; YOGA; EGYPTIAN DANCE; WALKING . . . RELAX AND REMEMBER THE WAY OF THE HAPPY CAT!

Handing in your Super Woman cape

Bree Van De Kamp must surely be the most desperate of Wisteria Lane's desperate housewives as she continually struggles to save face by hiding her emotions and controlling her behaviour. In an interview with the *Sunday Times Style* magazine, Marcia Cross, who plays the repressed Bree, has this to say: ' . . . I identify with her need to present a good front all the time . . . I think all women are taught from a young age to fit into this box.' Ms Cross, who has a degree in psychology, goes on to say that, 'There are a lot of women trying to be the perfect everything and trying to hide what they perceive to be their failures.' She thinks that Bree is such a popular character because so many women can relate to her obsessive personality.

Stop for a moment and think about how you relate to the need to present a good front; is this an issue for you? Could this be making you unhappy? If you are trying to have it all and be it all, then you will most probably also be having to do it all; this is the price you have to pay if you want to look like you are always in control. Sure, you can slow down a bit, adopt the more tranquil habits of the happy cat and make some personal lifestyle changes but none of these strategies will make much difference if you always need to keep a tight hold of the reins.

Take this great piece of advice from Dr Bost (the man who identified the Hurried Woman Syndrome) who says: 'Hand in your Super Woman cape and say, "I can't do everything to please everyone else anymore."'

CHANGE ONE THING

REVAMP YOUR TO-DO LIST

What, you haven't got one? Well, perhaps it's now time to get your plans down on paper rather than letting them play havoc in your head. Not having an itemised plan is a bit like going to the supermarket without a list; anything might find its way into our trolley as we wander down the aisles picking up whatever takes our fancy. Similarly anything can happen on a day when we know we have certain things to do but we can't quite remember what they are! This creates the unhappy feeling that we are out of control. So get your list together! And if you are already a consummate list maker then it might be time to revamp your approach. A to-do list will only make your life easier and happier if it is realistic; if it's not and it makes heavy demands on your time and energy then it will only become a burden.

Take your list and do this:

- Cross out all those things that are not at all urgent; they can wait for another day.

- Cross out all those things that you know you will never do but like to think you might.

- Don't fill the spaces with new items; you have just created some free time for you.

- Prioritise what you have left; number them with 1 being the most important.

- Do the things on your list in order of importance.

Do your own Happiness Audit

Our levels of happiness depend upon the quality of our moments so it's vital that we get to grips with how we actually spend our time. The Happiness Audit allows you to take a long hard look at how you allocate your time over the course of a typical day and whether it is well spent in terms of creating happiness for you. There are two parts to the Audit.

Part 1 First you create a life balance pie chart that represents the way you spend your hours in a day. You may of course need to draw more than one chart if the days in your week are drastically different. Michelle's pie chart is an example of how to set about this.

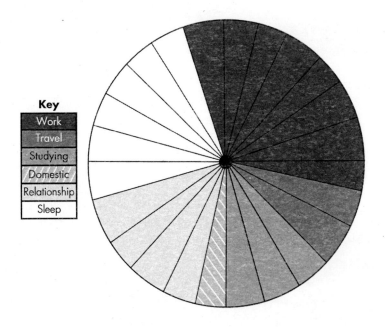

Key
- Work
- Travel
- Studying
- Domestic
- Relationship
- Sleep

MICHELLE'S LIFE BALANCE PIE CHART

Michelle is a 24-year-old student nurse who works an eight-hour day (often on different shifts). It takes an hour to get to the hospital where she works and she spend three hours a day studying. She lives with boyfriend Steve who is unemployed at the moment. Her pie chart represents the different 'categories' of time she spends in a usual day.

Now draw your own chart, using your own categories.

Part 2 The second part of the Audit takes your time-spent categories and evaluates them in terms of their happiness rating. Using the fed-up to fabulous scale give each of these items a score from 1 to 10.

TOTALLY FED-UP									FABULOUS
1	2	3	4	5	6	7	8	9	10

The happiness-rating table on page 56 shows how Michelle transferred her information from her pie chart and the insights she gained.

When you have completed your pie chart in your journal, translate your findings into your own happiness-rating table. Most people are quite astonished by what this table reveals to them. In my experience the whole audit acts like a laser beam, focusing on the quality of many aspects of our lives. When we get down to the nitty gritty and put our daily hours spent into this format it's almost impossible not to see things in a new light; surprising insights are revealed. We are then in a great position to see *exactly* what is making us happy/unhappy and creative new ideas may arise. Of course whether we decide to act on this information is entirely

MICHELLE'S HAPPINESS-RATING TABLE

CATEGORY	HOURS SPENT	HAPPINESS SCORE	WHY IT MAKES ME HAPPY / UNHAPPY	IDEAS ARISING
Sleep	6	3	am tired all the time, this makes me grumpy	must do something about this
Work	8	8.5	I love nursing - this will score 10 when have more qualifications	keep studying regularly
Travel	2	7	quite like this - can relax and listen to MP3 player or read on train	
Domestic	1	2	I end up doing most of the chores - very annoying	ask Steve to do more
Studying	3	7	don't mind this but it takes all my free time - would like to be able to relax a bit at night - might help me sleep	might go back to the yoga class
Relationship	4	5	can't believe this score - what is happening to us? I hate it that Steve is out of work - it is affecting us badly	Steve and I need a serious talk

down to us. In the meantime you could ask yourself these questions:

If I could free up some time what would I do with it?

What do I love doing and why?

What don't I like doing and why?

REFRESH AND RENEW

A SILENT RETREAT

SILENCE IS GOLDEN; IT OFFERS US A CALM AND PEACEFUL HAVEN AMIDST THE FRANTIC PACE OF DAILY LIFE. YOU DON'T HAVE TO BE 'ON' 24/7, YOU CAN STEP OUT FOR A WHILE ON A SILENT RETREAT.

- BEGIN BY CHANGING YOUR AWARENESS SLIGHTLY, SO THAT YOU FOCUS ON THE SPACES BETWEEN WORDS WHEN OTHERS ARE TALKING AROUND YOU. NOTICE HOW DIFFERENT TYPES OF SILENCE MEAN DIFFERENT THINGS IN COMMUNICATION.

- TRY KEEPING QUIET FOR AS LONG AS POSSIBLE WHEN IN COMPANY AND RECOGNISE WHEN YOU LONG TO JOIN IN WITH THE CHAT; STOP YOURSELF AND SEE HOW THIS FEELS.

- THINK OF SILENCE AS A SUPPORTIVE AND NURTURING CONDITION RATHER THAN JUST A LACK OF NOISE.

- HAVE A SILENT RETREAT EVERY DAY, EVEN IF YOU CAN ONLY MANAGE FIVE MINUTES. TURN OFF ALL NOISY DISTRACTIONS AND STOP TALKING.

- AS YOU PRACTISE BEING SILENT YOU WILL COME TO LOVE THIS STATE; LET SILENCE BE YOUR FRIEND.

Day 2 TODAY'S HAPPINESS ROUNDUP

It's time to gather together your thoughts about today in the happiness roundup. Do as you did yesterday, circle your happiness score and fill in the following sections in your journal.

MY HAPPINESS SCORE FOR THE DAY

TOTALLY   FABULOUS
FED-UP
    1   2   3   4   5   6   7   8   9   10

Most significant event of the day

....

....

My main concern of the day

....

....

What can I do about this, if anything?

....

....

Most useful happiness strategies today

....

....

What went well today

....

....

Three things that made me smile today

....

....

Add any extra thoughts and reflections that you have had today and take a look at the final reflections.

Final reflections

- There is more to life than increasing its speed.
- Enjoy the journey as well as the outcome and go the way of the happy cat.
- If you make your to-do lists more realistic you will feel more in control.
- You deserve to take time for yourself.
- Silence is golden; enjoy it whenever you can.

Become an Optimist

Optimism is an attitude that buffers people against falling into apathy, hopelessness, or depression in the face of tough going.

DANIEL GOLEMAN

An optimist is the human personification of spring.

Susan J. Bissonette

When my youngest child packed his bags to leave for university last September I felt very down in the dumps. Although I had been 'practising' for this moment for months nothing had prepared me for the quite the way I felt, and for a few weeks I lost sight of my sunny, positive, optimistic self (just when I needed her the most). And isn't this often what happens? When we are low and could do with a lift it can be very hard to find the optimism and hope that we need to buoy up our spirits and give us the strength to bounce back again.

Feeling fed-up didn't suit me; I didn't like it at all and, as you can imagine, I fought back with every tip and technique in the book (which in my case is rather a lot!). In the end I walked my way back to happiness. Instead of being there and missing Alex at the end of the school day I went for a stroll along a beautiful footpath that leads into town and soon it became a wonderful daily ritual. I walked past the trees as they lost their leaves and I enjoyed an amazing autumn, something which I had never quite had the time to appreciate before. And then it was winter and I loved the quiet bare branches and brisk cold days. And now it is spring, which surely must be the most optimistic of seasons, and those plucky snowdrops are bouncing back yet again.

The seasons inevitably take their natural course and there is comfort and security in the recognition of these cycles. We also go through natural cycles of change but at times these are harder for us to come to terms with. If you are going through any type of grieving process right now (dealing with a death, relationship break-up or other significant loss) then you need to know that these difficult feelings will pass; everything changes and your emotional state will too. Sometimes we just have to wait in optimistic hopefulness for the dark clouds to blow over. It is utterly meaningless and unhelpful to be told not to worry and to 'be happy' when our mood is very low.

However, an optimistic stance always works wonderfully well at many levels. In the short term this might just mean changing a negative attitude to a more positive one but in the long term optimism builds the inner strength and resilience that keep us hopeful and upbeat in the face of life's inevitable challenges. Writing in *Psychologies* magazine, Dr Nick Bayliss, a positive psychologist at Cambridge University, had this to say: 'Optimism means taking the attitude that things will improve if we just put some effort in. This highly learnable attitude to everyday life is widely regarded by psychologists as one of the most beneficial personality characteristics – hundreds of studies demonstrate that optimists are not only higher achievers, both at work and on the playing field, but they also enjoy better physical health, faster recovery from illness, and suffer much less anxiety and depression.' Plenty of good reasons to get learning the optimistic habit then!

CHANGE ONE THING

BY GETTING READY FOR SUCCESS

SOMETIMES AN IMMEDIATE CHANGE IN ATTITUDE IS ALL IT TAKES TO TURN A NEGATIVE PESSIMISTIC FEELING INTO A POSITIVE AND OPTIMISTIC ONE.

- NEXT TIME YOU FIND YOURSELF VISUALISING THE WORST POSSIBLE OUTCOME BECOME AWARE OF WHAT YOU ARE DOING.
- AWARENESS IS ALWAYS THE FIRST STEP TO CHANGE. SO ONCE YOU REALISE THAT YOU ARE GOING DOWN A GLOOMY PATH, JUST STOP IT; REFUSE TO GO THERE.
- IMAGINE THE VERY BEST SCENARIO AND VISUALISE THAT INSTEAD. SEE IT HAPPENING AND MAKE IT ALL AS REAL AS POSSIBLE.
- NOW NOTICE THE DIFFERENCE BETWEEN HOW YOU FEEL WITH THE TWO DIFFERENT ATTITUDES.
- YES, YOUR OPTIMISTIC VIEW WILL MAKE YOU FEEL MUCH MORE UPBEAT, BUT ALSO REMEMBER THAT SUCCESSFUL THOUGHTS ATTRACT SUCCESS. SO THE OPTIMISTIC PATH IS REALLY THE ONLY VIABLE WAY TO GO!

Why pessimism makes us unhappy

And if you are thinking that a healthy degree of pessimism is a much more realistic approach then think again. A client once described himself to me as a 'pessimistic realist'. He said that focusing on the worst-case scenario was always the safest option for him because he then knew that he could never be disappointed. Naturally I took issue with this strange logic, particularly because he wanted coaching to increase his confidence and levels of happiness. We can never be happy if we are playing the pessimistic card. If you have ever found yourself expecting the worst in order to protect yourself from disappointment you will know that this strategy doesn't work. Well yes, if I am convinced that I would never get the fabulous promotion that's on offer and I don't, then I will have proved myself right, but what will I have achieved? However, if I had gone for that promotion in an optimistic and upbeat manner then who knows what might have happened?

But research suggests that if we expect failure then we will actually attract failure. Discussing the pitfalls of pessimism in the *Psychologies* article, Nick Bayliss suggests that, although we might think it sensible to consider all the negative possibilities this is not actually a useful strategy. He says that: 'Though we tell ourselves we'll look at the negative "what ifs" just to be on the safe side and then return quickly to the positives, our brain has evolved to err towards "high alert" and neuroticism, so we all too easily get stuck in the doom and gloom gear. In trying to predict what bad things might happen, we can inadvertently bring the bad things into being. Studies have shown that pessimism leads to a fatalistic attitude to life.' Homer Simpson humorously takes the defeatist's position to the absolute limit by concluding that: 'Trying is the first step to failure.'

Perhaps you think that you are stuck in the gloom and doom gear because you are a natural pessimist. If you find it difficult to lighten your load, be heartened by the fact that optimism is a skill that you can learn. Psychologists have proved the amazing benefits of teaching the techniques of optimism. For example, in the famous Penn Prevention Program, troubled children were taught ways to deal with tough challenges with optimism. At the end of the programme the total number of them who were suffering with depressive symptoms had fallen by 35 per cent. And after two years all of them had beaten their depression.

Checking out your optimistic/pessimistic tendencies

To each and every life experience you bring your whole self: your mind, body, spirit and emotions. This means that your *thoughts*, *feelings* and *actions* exist simultaneously and that they are connected; they affect each other and in fact help to create each other.

Imagine having the thought that you are doing really well at something (*wow, I'm making a great job of this*). Your feelings will be directly affected by this thought (*I'm feeling great, full of enthusiasm*) and your actions will reflect your thoughts and feelings (you will put your whole heart into whatever you are doing and give it all you've got). Can you see how each aspect of your being is interconnected?

Now imagine that you have just given a great presentation at work. Your successful actions will give rise to feelings of confidence and your thoughts and beliefs about yourself will be positive. Our thoughts, feelings and actions co-create each other and are mutually dependent, and this means that if we change the quality of any of these three aspects it will directly affect the other two. Take a look at the next diagram, which demonstrates how this interdependency works to create each of our experiences.

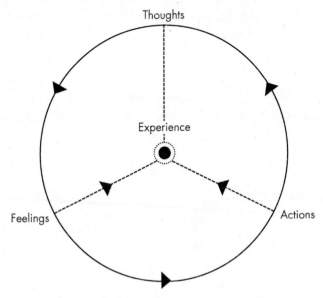

AN INTERCONNECTED EXPERIENCE

And if you are still wondering if you are more doomful than hopeful, then take a look at the table on page 69, which assesses some of the thoughts, feelings and actions of the pessimist and the optimist.

ARE YOU AN OPTIMIST OR A PESSIMIST?

	THE OPTIMIST	THE PESSIMIST
THINKS:	THINGS USUALLY WORK OUT FOR ME	IF SOMETHING CAN GO WRONG IT WILL
	I AM OFTEN LUCKY	I AM AN UNLUCKY PERSON
	I CREATE MY OWN HAPPINESS	I AM UNABLE TO CHANGE MY MOODS
	WHEN BAD THINGS HAPPEN I KNOW THAT I WILL COPE	WHEN BAD THINGS HAPPEN IT DEVASTATES ME
	MOST PEOPLE MEAN WELL	EVERYONE IS LOOKING OUT FOR THEMSELVES
FEELS:	APPRECIATIVE MOST OF THE TIME	THAT THERE IS NOT MUCH TO LOOK FORWARD TO
	LARGELY IN CONTROL	LARGELY OUT OF CONTROL
	IN TOUCH WITH OWN EMOTIONS	OUT OF TOUCH WITH OWN EMOTIONS
	CONFIDENT	LOW IN CONFIDENCE
	BUOYANT	FLAT
ACTS:	ASSERTIVELY	PASSIVELY/AGGRESSIVELY
	TRUSTINGLY	CRITICALLY
	WITH PERSEVERANCE AND FOCUS IN THE FACE OF DIFFICULTY	WITHOUT INNER STRENGTH WHEN THE GOING GETS ROUGH
	WITH GOOD COMMUNICATION SKILLS	WITH POOR COMMUNICATION SKILLS
	OPENLY	DEFENSIVELY

Dealing with your inner Eeyore – using cognitive therapy

I love the following extract from *The Pooh Book of Quotations* by A.A. Milne:

The old grey donkey, Eeyore stood by himself in a thistly corner of the Forest, his front feet well apart, his head on one side, and thought about things. Sometimes he thought sadly to himself, 'Why?' and sometimes he thought, 'Wherefore?' and sometimes he thought, 'Inasmuch as which?' and sometimes he didn't quite know what he was thinking about.

Just like Eeyore, we can so easily let our thoughts run away with themselves so that they take us on a ponderous journey through increasingly gloomy and perplexing tunnels of worry and doubt. It's easy to relate to that feeling of not knowing quite what we are thinking, and when this happens we really are at the mercy of our mental processes.

Our thoughts have such a powerful effect on us; they can make us feel fed-up or fabulous and anything else in between. Cognitive therapy is a very popular and extremely well researched form of psychotherapy and its principles are very simple. Cognitive therapists recognise that our daily reality is actually the by-product of how we perceive it, with specific errors in thinking producing specific problems. Similarly if we change our thinking we can produce alternative outcomes. This is how the process works in theory:

A (event) → **B** (thoughts about event) → **C** (emotions resulting from thought processes)

Now take a look at this example:

A (my partner leaves) → **B** (I think I am worthless, no one will ever love me again) → **C** (I feel lost and depressed)

To lift our mood we can use the principles of cognitive therapy to look closely and realistically at the negative thoughts that are leading to our unhappiness. In the example above I could challenge the belief that I am worthless and that no one will ever love me again; these thoughts are based on cognitive distortions and they are making me miserable. Once I can see that these thoughts are not really true then I can take a more positive line, which immediately leads to a happier mood.

Psychologist Dr Aaron Beck suggested that an ongoing sad mood and lack of motivation are the result of cognitive distortions based on certain beliefs about the world, the future and ourselves. For example, if I view the world as an unfair and hard place to be then it will seem impossible to me that I could ever feel comfortable and happy. And if I feel there is no hope for the future then I cannot imagine how I can overcome my present difficulties. My beliefs about myself will also have a big impact on my mood: if I feel inadequate, alone and 'not good enough', then I will certainly find it hard to generate any enthusiasm.

ACTIVITY: LOOKING AT MY MOST POSITIVE FEATURES

PERHAPS YOU HAVE NEVER REALLY THOUGHT ABOUT THE WAY YOU SEE YOURSELF, BUT YOUR 'SELF-CONCEPT' DETERMINES HOW YOU PRESENT YOURSELF TO THE WORLD. AND IT ALSO AFFECTS HOW THE REST OF THE WORLD RELATES TO YOU. IF YOUR SELF-CONCEPT IS RIDDLED WITH NEGATIVITY THEN YOU WILL FEEL UNHAPPY A LOT OF THE

TIME AND YOUR MOOD WILL BE DOWNBEAT AND PESSIMISTIC. HOWEVER AS SOON AS YOU CHANGE YOUR SELF-CONCEPT SO THAT YOU SEE YOURSELF IN A MORE POSITIVE LIGHT YOUR LIFE WILL LOOK BRIGHTER, HAPPIER AND MORE HOPEFUL.

STEP 1 THINK OF 5 THINGS THAT YOU DON'T LIKE ABOUT YOURSELF.

STEP 2 NOW THINK OF 5 THINGS THAT YOU DO LIKE ABOUT YOURSELF.

WHEN I ASK PEOPLE TO DO THIS THEY USUALLY FINISH STEP 1 VERY QUICKLY AND THEN FIND THEMSELVES STRUGGLING WITH STEP 2. WE ARE PRETTY HARD ON OURSELVES AND ARE OFTEN OUR OWN BIGGEST CRITICS, BUT THIS CAN LEAD TO A POOR SELF-CONCEPT AND POOR RELATIONSHIPS WITH OTHERS.

LIFT YOUR SELF-CONCEPT BY CREATING A LIST OF YOUR MOST POSITIVE FEATURES. START WITH THE FIVE YOU HAVE ALREADY AND KEEP ADDING TO IT. PUT THIS LIST IN A VISIBLE PLACE SO THAT YOU ARE CONTINUALLY REMINDED OF HOW FAB YOU REALLY ARE. AND IF YOU ARE THINKING THAT IT DOESN'T BECOME YOU TO BUILD YOURSELF UP IN THIS WAY, TAKE HEED: YOUR HAPPINESS MIGHT BE AT STAKE. IF YOU BRING YOURSELF DOWN THEN OTHERS WILL SOON BEGIN TO AGREE WITH YOUR DEFINITION OF WHO YOU ARE. THINK WELL OF YOURSELF AND OTHERS WILL RESPOND BY THINKING WELL OF YOU.

From Eeyore to Tigger

The irrepressible Tigger bounces into the spotlight in the Disney classic, *The Tigger Movie,* made in 2000. I had the great good fortune to see this movie with my granddaughter Alaska and we both rate it as one of our favourite films. We bounced out of the cinema full of Tiggerisms and optimism and this effect served to reinforce my belief that optimism is contagious!

Compare that soulful and doleful quote from Eeyore (page 71) with these words of wisdom from Tigger, taken from the movie. 'The most wonderful thing about tiggers, is that tiggers are a wonderful thing, they are bouncy, trouncy, pouncy, and lots of fun, fun, fun!'

I don't know about you but I am not so interested in hanging about in the thistle patch ruminating sadly and worriedly; I would much prefer to be having fun, fun, fun and yet more fun!

Cognitive therapy offers such an easy way for us to understand how we create either an optimistic or pessimistic outlook. Aaron Beck identified certain specific cognitive distortions that lead to psychological problems. In other words, he looked at the ways that specific types of negative thinking lead to low spirits and unhappiness. Once we become aware of the thinking patterns that don't work for us we can then choose to change our harmful thoughts by thinking in a new and optimistic way.

5 ways to change from a pessimist to an optimist

1   **Stop catastrophising.** Catastrophising is psychology speak for making a mountain out of a molehill. When we

look for everything that can go wrong we stop seeing the possibilities in a situation and this leads to inaction, lack of clarity and, of course, unhappiness.

Example: I have been given a new project at work and I realise that I have missed out an important piece of information in my first report, which I have already emailed to my boss. I get into a terrible state imagining that I will lose the contract and that I might even lose my job.

The way of the optimist: To stop assuming the worst so that I can think my way out of the situation, perhaps by considering how I can add the new information as an appendix to my report.

2 **Look for the middle way.** Under stress we are inclined to think in extremes: things can seem very black and white with very little room for movement in between.

Example: My boyfriend forgets to ring me on my birthday and I immediately assume that he doesn't love me any more and that our relationship is over.

The way of the optimist: To look at the grey area in between which gives rise to another possibility: it is more than likely that he has just forgotten!

3 **Don't jump to conclusions.** Dr Beck describes how we can draw erroneous conclusions by basing our understanding on inaccurate or incomplete thinking. And he gives us a graphic illustration.

Example: He says that if two scientists are asked to describe an elephant but they can only see it through a small hole in the fence they are likely to come up with different descriptions. One might see the tail and rightly deduce that the elephant is an animal with a tail and the other might see only the trunk and make a similar incomplete judgement.

The way of the optimist: To make sure that I have as many facts as possible at my disposal before I come to a conclusion in any situation. Once I have done my research I will know that I am in a position to make the best possible decision.

4   **Stop generalising.** We do this when we take an isolated experience and apply it to other unconnected areas of our life.

Example: Because I failed that exam it means that there is no point in me ever studying for any new qualifications.

The way of the optimist: To look at the logic of the situation and to know that my conclusion is not true; it is a deeply pessimistic response which is not grounded in reality and it only serves to make me even more unhappy. Why should I let one mistake stand in my way?

5   **Keep things in context.** Dr Beck described the negative thinking that leads to us getting things out of context and gives the following illustration.

Example: A male college student believed that women always laughed at him when they walked past him. Little did he know that most of the women were not even aware of him and that they were only laughing at a joke or some funny situation that had nothing to do with him.

The way of the optimist: To keep a positive approach and not to take behaviour out of context. Negative abstractions are pessimistic imaginings and they only create misery and sadness.

Catch that pessimistic thought

The difference between optimism and pessimism is only a thought away. But what exactly is that thought which stands between a happy positive outlook and an unhappy miserable one? When clients struggle to maintain a sunny disposition I often use a really simple and yet incredibly effective technique, which I call thought-catching. It takes just 5 easy steps to accomplish.

Step 1   Start to notice that thoughts are continually running through your mind. This might come as a bit of a surprise at first but that mind of yours never does stop chattering!

Step 2   Notice any negative and self-defeating thoughts. Do this in a non-critical way so that you don't blame yourself and become even unhappier. One way to do this is to imagine these thoughts as butterflies and see yourself catching them in a net.

Step 3   Scrutinise your catch; what are these self-doubts and limiting beliefs that take your mood down?

Step 4   Identify each negative thought and replace it with a contradictory positive message.

Step 5   Now visualise those negative-making butterflies flying away.

Cheryl's story

Cheryl, 36, has a high-powered job in the City. Two months ago she met Martin, an IT consultant, and they began a fabulous relationship. Meanwhile, Cheryl had been offered a great promotion at work. Now why do you think Cheryl would have wanted life coaching?

She had consulted me because she was so terrified that all the good things that had happened to her were going to fall apart; she became convinced that something bad was about to happen at any time and she was very unhappy. Her mood affected her relationship and Martin thought that she didn't want to see him any more and things got difficult between them. At work Cheryl began to worry that her colleagues might be jealous of her success and she stopped enjoying her job.

It is not unusual for us to find it hard to embrace the good; sometimes we just don't think we deserve it and we look for any way to sabotage our progress. When this happens we need to do some thought-catching. Cheryl began the 5-step plan described above. She worked on this for a week and when we next spoke she had this to say: 'Well, to start with I couldn't believe the way that thoughts keep rushing through my mind. Then I began to pick out the negative ones and I was shocked by how I kept frightening myself with worrying thoughts about the future. Then I started to look closely at the negative thoughts and I wrote them down. When I was with Martin I heard myself thinking *this will never last* and *I can't be this happy*. I also noticed that I was always surprised when he did what he said he was going to do and I realised that I find it hard to trust that things can be OK with a man.'

We talked for a while about Cheryl's early years with her parents and she told me that although her father was fairly optimistic her mother was very afraid of life and became quite withdrawn. When Cheryl went to university in London her mother rang her every day because she was so worried about her safety. And then last year her mother's worst nightmares came true when Cheryl's father left her for another woman.

After this discussion Cheryl recognised that she was just repeating some of her mother's pessimistic patterns and she resolved to work on letting those butterflies fly away. Cheryl created a list of positively affirming and optimistic beliefs to replace the old negative ones. She used the following affirmations:

I deserve to be happy
My life is wonderful
I am good at my job
I love my job
I deserve promotion
Life is fun
I am loveable
I can be happy

She worked hard to change her limiting negative beliefs and soon started to lift out of the downward pessimistic spiral and began to appreciate her wonderful good fortune.

Try creating your own list of positive affirmations that challenge any of your negative beliefs. Write them on brightly coloured stick-on notes and put them all around the house, in your car and at work. Surround yourself with a positive and optimistic vibration and just feel your energy rise.

CHANGE ONE THING

BY FOCUSING ON THE BEST POSSIBILITY

WE KNOW THAT A POSITIVE APPROACH ALWAYS ENCOURAGES THE BEST POSSIBLE OUTCOME (AS WELL AS MAKING US FEEL HAPPY). TRY THE FOLLOWING TASK. A SIMPLE EXAMPLE SHOWS HOW IT WORKS.

1 CONSIDER ANY CHALLENGING DECISION THAT YOU ARE FACING AT THE MOMENT.

EXAMPLE: *I AM NOT SURE WHETHER TO MOVE OUT OF THE TOWN.*

2 NOW COMPLETE THE FOLLOWING SENTENCE: WHEN I FOCUS ON THE BEST POSSIBLE OUTCOME I FEEL ....

EXAMPLE: . . . *VERY EXCITED BY THE PROSPECT OF LIVING IN THE COUNTRYSIDE, HAVING A GARDEN AND SLOWING DOWN MY FRANTIC PACE.*

3 WHEN YOUR THOUGHTS AND FEELINGS ARE OPTIMISTIC YOUR ACTIONS WILL BECOME CLEARLY FOCUSED; YOU WILL *KNOW* JUST WHAT YOU NEED TO DO. TO ACTIVATE THIS I NEED TO..

> EXAMPLE: . . . *START LOOKING FOR A NEW PROPERTY, CONTACT ESTATE AGENTS AND PUT MY HOUSE ON THE MARKET.*
>
> OPTIMISTS CAN TRANSLATE POSITIVE THOUGHTS AND FEELINGS INTO POSITIVE AND ASSERTIVE ACTION.

Your reasons to be optimistic

Self-help guru Steven Covey said that: 'As long as you think the problem is out there, that very thought is the problem.' In other words, a negative thought creates a negative reality. One way to encourage yourself to turn away from pessimism towards optimism is to make a realistic inventory of the good aspects of your life. You have so many reasons to be positive but sometimes you might just forget them. Write a list to remind you, using the following categories.

Think of . . . . . .
- Someone who loves you
- Someone you love
- A personal strength
- Your favourite food
- A time when you showed kindness to someone
- The very best thing that happened this week
- A time when someone showed kindness to you
- Something that you do very well
- One thing you like about where you are living
- A moment when you felt appreciated
- A reason to be proud of yourself

Go back to this list whenever you need to be reminded of some of the good things in your life. Revise it when necessary and add any other categories that come to mind.

Optimism creates happiness and happiness creates optimism, and this positive choice is one that you can always take. I know life can be hard and we can lose our good spirits for a while but optimists are resilient; like Tigger, they bounce back and they don't let anything grind them down. Next time you are in a difficult place on life's journey try taking a step back from your emotions and ask yourself what would be the most optimistic approach for you. Remember that a positive attitude will always attract the best possible outcome, so expect the best and you will get the best.

REFRESH AND RENEW

PEACE IN YOUR MIND
PEACE IN YOUR HEART

WHEN YOU ARE CENTRED AND CALM YOUR BREATHING DEEPENS AND SLOWS DOWN; YOUR THOUGHTS NO LONGER PREOCCUPY YOU AND YOUR HEART FEELS FULL OF LOVE AND HAPPINESS. TRY THIS WONDERFUL MEDITATION TO CALM YOUR THOUGHTS AND YOUR EMOTIONS.

- SIT DOWN, RELAX AND CLOSE YOUR EYES.
- FOLLOW YOUR BREATHING FOR A FEW MOMENTS UNTIL IT BECOMES DEEPER AND SLOWER. WHEN THIS HAPPENS YOUR BODY WILL SPONTANEOUSLY LET GO OF TENSION.
- NOW SAY TO YOURSELF, 'MAY MY MIND BE FULL OF PEACE.' AS YOU SAY THIS IMAGINE A BEAUTIFUL WHITE LIGHT FILLING YOUR BODY WITH UPLIFTING ENERGY. BATHE IN THIS LIGHT FOR A FEW MOMENTS.
- AND THEN SAY TO YOURSELF, 'MAY MY HEART BE FULL OF PEACE.' AS YOU SAY THIS VISUALISE A BEAUTIFUL

PINK LIGHT FILLING YOUR HEART WITH GLADNESS. REST IN THIS BEAUTIFUL PLACE FOR A FEW MOMENTS.

WHEN YOU ARE READY, OPEN YOUR EYES AND SLOWLY BRING YOURSELF BACK INTO THE ROOM. THIS LITTLE MEDITATION IS LIKE A REFRESHING BALM TO OUR SPIRIT AND IT IS SO EASY TO DO. IF IT'S NOT PRACTICAL TO CLOSE YOUR EYES (YOU ARE AT WORK OR ON THE TUBE OR WALKING DOWN THE STREET) JUST SAY THE WORDS TO YOURSELF AND IMAGINE THE BEAUTIFUL WHITE LIGHT FILLING YOUR THOUGHTS AND THE PINK LIGHT FILLING YOUR HEART. LET THESE WORDS BECOME A MANTRA TO CREATE AN OASIS OF CALM FOR YOU WHEREVER YOU ARE:

MAY MY MIND BE FULL OF PEACE
MAY MY HEART BE FULL OF PEACE

Day 3 TODAY'S HAPPINESS ROUNDUP

And now collect together your thoughts and ideas about today in the happiness roundup. Circle your happiness score and fill out the appropriate sections in your journal.

MY HAPPINESS SCORE FOR THE DAY

TOTALLY   FABULOUS
FED-UP
   1   2   3   4   5   6   7   8   9   10

Most significant event of the day

....

....

My main concern of the day

....

....

What can I do about this, if anything?

....

....

Most useful happiness strategies today

....

....

What went well today

....

....

Three things that made me smile today

....

....

Now add anything else that has been significant today.

Final reflections

- Optimism is a skill that can we can learn.
- Optimists are winners in all aspects of life.
- You can change the way you feel by changing the way you think.
- Positivity and optimism generate happiness.
- You have so many reasons to be optimistic.

Day 4
Moving On

We are what we think.
All that we are arises with our thoughts.
With our thoughts we make the world.

THE BUDDHA

To effect a change you have to change your thinking. Realising that was a revelation to me and I'm in the process of trying to do it. I'm viewing my situation and my place in the world with different eyes. I hope I keep this change in my train of thought because it is beneficial to me and I actually feel happier. I feel lifted.

Positive psychology tells us that we can teach ourselves to be happy. This 'science of happiness' has its roots in research that shows that childhood experiences and genetic traits account for only 50 per cent of our happiness potential and that we have control of the rest. It has also been shown that those who describe themselves as 'very happy' are no more beautiful, sociable or successful than the average person. So what does make the vital difference between those who consider themselves happy and those who don't? Well, the social scientists claim that the happy bunnies amongst us have taken two vital steps:

Step 1 We have discovered what makes us happy.
Step 2 We have included more of these happiness-making activities in our lives.

MOVING ON | 87

I know, this sounds like ordinary common sense, but reflect on these two steps for a moment. Do you know what you love to do? Are you doing what makes you happy or are you pursuing an unhappy-making path? Are your life choices defined by you or do you feel limited by the wishes and needs of others? Although you know that the optimistic approach creates happiness do you sometimes choose a more pessimistic attitude? And do you let negative patterns drag you down or are you fighting back with positive affirmations and assertive action?

We can only take these two steps if we *know* what makes us happy and if we are prepared to make the changes needed to bring more of this quality into our lives.

Fifty volunteers, who wished to experience greater levels of happiness, were chosen from Slough (UK), to participate in a unique experiment that was filmed and shown as the television series *Making Slough Happy* on BBC2 in 2005. The series showed how it is possible for ordinary people, just like you and me, to bring a new level of joy into their lives. The programme's happiness experts combined a theoretical approach with simple practical experiments and community-based activities and demonstrated quite clearly that if we do more of what makes us happy we will of course feel happier!

CHANGE ONE THING

BY DOING SOMETHING THAT YOU LOVE

I OFTEN ASK CLIENTS TO TELL ME THE THINGS THEY USED TO LOVE TO DO TEN YEARS AGO BUT DON'T DO ANY MORE. THIS LIST IS OFTEN QUITE A REVEALING REMINDER OF LONG-FORGOTTEN PLEASURABLE ACTIVITIES.

- THINK BACK TO THE PAST AND REMEMBER SOME OF THE THINGS YOU LOVED TO DO.

- WHY HAVE YOU STOPPED DOING THEM?

- CHOOSE ONE ITEM FROM THIS LIST THAT YOU COULD DO THIS WEEK.

- DECIDE WHEN YOU WILL DO IT AND WRITE IT IN YOUR DIARY.

- THEN JUST DO IT!

MAKE TIME FOR PLEASURE AND LET PRIORITISING HAPPINESS BECOME ONE OF YOUR NEW DAILY HABITS.

Raise the bar for yourself

Liz Hoggard, who wrote a book about the Slough experiment called *How to be Happy*, reminds us of something very important: 'Remember, happiness is good for you, so don't be embarrassed about making it a priority. But finding it is not a competition. Authentic happiness derives from raising the bar for yourself, not rating yourself against others. A joyful life is an individual creation that cannot be copied from a recipe.'

We all deserve to be happy but we don't always believe this, do we? We get what we expect. What do you expect for yourself? What do you think you deserve? Think about your answers. Are your beliefs creating limitations for you? If for some reason you think you don't deserve to be happy then you will find every reason under the sun to stay in Eeyore's negative thistle patch.

Raising the bar for yourself will bring positive changes for you but you will have to be prepared to leave some of your oh so comfortable habits behind. I have nothing against the odd comfort zone (we all need the security of the familiar) but we have to be flexible enough to change and move on as the need arises. Nothing stays the same and you are changing, progressing and developing every day, and if you don't move with the times then you will begin to feel stuck, indecisive, low in confidence and unhappy. Yes, change can feel threatening and risky but no change can feel even worse. If you are feeling stuck in any area of your life then this will undoubtedly affect your levels of happiness. Look at the following list to see what changes you can make so that you can move forward, take control and feel happy again.

20 ways to move onwards and upwards

1   Know that you deserve the best.
2   Allow yourself to be happy.
3   Be confident and trust yourself.
4   When opportunity knocks, answer the door.
5   Feel the fear and do it anyway.
6   Reframe your experience by seeing problems as challenges.
7   Be courageous and you will fill yourself with positive energy.
8   Welcome change and go with it.
9   Learn from your mistakes and move on.
10   Ditch any feelings of guilt; they will hold you back forever.
11   Make a decision and follow it through.
12   Be prepared to jump over obstacles.
13   Visualise a great outcome.

14   Remember that you are good enough just the way you are.

15   Let go of negative thoughts.

16   Believe in your happy future.

17   Smile in the face of uncertainty.

18   Let yourself be the best you can be.

19   Enjoy the success of others.

20   Trust your gut feelings.

HAPPINESS TIP

KEEP YOUR SPIRITS UP

NEXT TIME YOU FEEL THE NEED TO MOAN AND COMPLAIN ABOUT SOMETHING STOP AND REMEMBER THAT: THE MORE YOU TALK ABOUT A NEGATIVE EFFECT THE MORE POWER IT HAS OVER YOU. OF COURSE IF SOMETHING NEEDS CHANGING YOU CAN STATE THAT FACT BUT THE NEXT STEP MUST BE TO DO SOMETHING ABOUT IT. REPEATED COMPLAINTS ARE MERELY NEGATIVE AFFIRMATIONS AND THESE CAN EASILY BECOME UNCONSCIOUS HABITS OF SPEECH. THEIR EFFECT IS TO LOWER OUR POSITIVE ENERGY AND THE ENERGY OF ALL OF THOSE AROUND US (NOT A HAPPY-MAKING PROSPECT). WHEN YOU NEXT FEEL THE URGE TO GRUMBLE, DO THIS:

• AS YOU BECOME AWARE OF THE GRUMBLING PATH THAT YOU ARE ABOUT TO TAKE, STOP IMMEDIATELY.

• ASK YOURSELF IF YOU CAN DO ANYTHING ABOUT THIS UNFAVOURABLE SITUATION.

- IF YOU CAN, THEN WHAT ARE YOU WAITING FOR, ACT NOW.

- AND IF YOU CAN'T, THEN RECOGNISE THAT YOU HAVE NOTHING TO GAIN BY COMPLAINING EXCEPT AN INCREASINGLY NEGATIVE SPIRIT.

PEOPLE IN THE UK OFTEN COMPLAIN A LOT ABOUT THE WEATHER. AS THERE IS NOTHING WHATEVER THAT WE CAN DO TO CHANGE IT WHY BOTHER TO WASTE OUR GOOD SPIRITS BY BECOMING VICTIMS TO A DROP OF RAIN?

A positive look at our 'problems'

When clients tell me that they are feeling unhappy I always take a positive stance (of course!). The stories we tell about our misery and sadness can sometimes trap us in negativity. Have you ever found yourself rehearsing a speech about your 'problems' that you intend to tell someone else? Or perhaps you have heard yourself repeating a litany of complaints verbatim. This dwelling on the past never makes us feel good and only serves to depress those around us. I'm sure you know people who are constantly grumbling; they seem to be able to suck the positivity out of the very air around us and leave us feeling flat and gasping for a laugh. These people are energy vampires and they are happy to be unhappy – stay away from them!

Cognitive therapy works by challenging our thoughts about the present and helping us to set future goals while brief solution-focused therapy (a new branch of positive psychology) actively discourages any talk about 'problems' and helps us to recognise our own resources and strengths so that we feel empowered to make positive changes.

I always see unhappiness as a positive sign that the time has come to move on in some way. When you have grown out of a situation or a relationship you will naturally feel discontented. But if you view this as a normal process it is much easier to understand the dynamics of what is going on and then to make the necessary changes. Don't be afraid of change; be proactive and instead of just sitting and waiting for something to happen begin to create the outcomes that you desire.

If you were a client of mine who was feeling low I would tell you to stop dwelling on your 'problems' and instead to visualise yourself at a crossroads; in some way you have moved on from a situation and it's time to make some new decisions. How exciting! We would then look at your choice of paths and you would write their names on the signposts. I find this a great way for a client to open the doors to change. And then, easy does it, one step at a time.

No one knows you better than you know yourself. Trust your judgement and trust your feelings because they reflect your deepest needs. If you are unhappy then something needs to change and only you can do this. Make your happiness your priority; you deserve it.

A happy heart makes wise decisions

In a recent magazine interview, Olympic heptathlon champion Denise Lewis said: 'I am not Joan of Arc. I have moments of self-doubt. But when questions are spinning around in my head, I listen to my heart.' Whenever we are not at our bubbly confident best it's good to be mindful that others also suffer with issues of self-doubt. The reality is that we all have times when we struggle with our self-belief and when this happens we need to hold fast and hang on to our hats until the emotional dip is over. When the inner turbulence is past and we start to wonder what we should be doing the answers are often not where we look for them; we think and think but this frequently leads to more confusion. What great advice Denise gives when she suggests that we listen to our hearts. Try this tip now with any difficult situation that you are trying to resolve. Move your focus from your mind (trying to think everything through) and turn it to your heart. Ask yourself how you are really feeling and what would make you happy. Take the first answer that reveals itself and follow this through.

ACTIVITY: MAKING POSITIVE CHANGES IN MY LIFE

CHANGE CAN FEEL CONFUSING BECAUSE IT CAN BE THRILLING AND FRIGHTENING AT THE SAME TIME. ONE MOMENT WE MIGHT FEEL THAT, YES I CAN GO FOR THIS, AND THE NEXT MOMENT CAN FIND US SHIVERING IN OUR BOOTS. THIS MIXED BAG OF FEELINGS IS ENTIRELY NORMAL. TRY THIS EXERCISE, WHICH WILL HELP YOU TO OVERCOME ANY FEARS YOU MIGHT HAVE ABOUT ACTIVATING YOUR GREAT NEW FUTURE GOALS.

- THINK OF A WONDERFUL POSITIVE MOVE THAT YOU MADE THAT CHANGED YOUR LIFE SIGNIFICANTLY.

- RETRACE YOUR EMOTIONS AND REMEMBER WHAT IT FELT LIKE TO BE STANDING AT THE CROSSROADS OF CHANGE.

- HOW DID YOU OVERCOME YOUR NATURAL FEELINGS OF UNCERTAINTY? PERHAPS YOU FOLLOWED YOUR INSTINCTS OR MAYBE THERE WAS NO OTHER ALTERNATIVE TO TAKE.

- CREATE THAT MOMENT OF DECISIVENESS AGAIN. FEEL THAT POWERFUL SURGE OF KNOWING THAT YOU WERE MAKING A NEW POSITIVE CHOICE.

- REALLY GET INTO THE SKIN OF THAT FEELING NOW AND FEEL YOUR HAPPY AND OPTIMISTIC ENERGY.

- KEEP HOLD OF THIS FEELING WHILST YOU CONSIDER ANY NEW CHANGES THAT ARE ON YOUR HORIZON.

- STAND AT YOUR NEW CROSSROADS OF CHANGE AND KNOW THAT YOU WILL MAKE ALL THE RIGHT MOVES AT THE RIGHT TIME. YOU SEE, YOU HAVE DONE IT BEFORE AND YOU CAN DO IT AGAIN.

Choosing happiness

Have you ever been in a situation where it seems that if you get what you want then it means that someone else loses out? Don't forget what Liz Hoggard said about finding happiness; it isn't a competition. There are no real limitations on how happy we can be because happiness is a feeling that we find within ourselves. And although it might sometimes seem that we are in an I win-you lose or you win-I lose scenario this is never the case in the long run. Think of your happiness as an all-win situation: if you are feeling great then you will spread your good feelings around and everyone will benefit. Remember that you cannot take away another person's happiness and no one can take away yours. The following story demonstrates how even the seemingly worst-case scenario can be healed with happiness.

Dawn's and Clare's story

Dawn and Clare are in their late twenties and have been friends since schooldays. After university they both went to work in London and they shared a flat in Islington. Dawn works in publishing and Clare is in advertising and they fell for the same man. Martin worked with Clare and they started to date a couple of years ago. The three of them often went out together when Dawn was without a date, and one weekend when Clare was on a training course Martin and Dawn had dinner together. Dawn realised how much she liked Martin and found herself torn between her feelings for him and her friendship with Clare. When Dawn came for coaching she said that she was in an 'impossible' situation because if she declared her feelings for Martin then she would lose her friendship with Clare. I remember her saying to me, 'We can't all be happy.'

I asked her what was most important to her and she said that she couldn't give up Martin even if it meant losing Clare's friendship. Martin had similar strong feelings but also felt very badly about telling Clare. In the end they told Clare together and she was very upset, she moved out of the flat, changed her job and lost touch with Dawn and Martin for a few months. Just after they got engaged they met Clare at a party and she was pleased to see them, she had a new job that she loved and was having a great relationship with another man. She said to Dawn that although she had felt hurt for a while she eventually realised that Martin and Dawn made a great couple and that they were obviously meant to be together. Now they are all great friends again and Clare is godmother to their baby daughter. Yes, Clare was unhappy for a while, but then she was able to let go and move on and find happiness for herself again.

When following your happiness seems to have a negative effect on another person it can be hard to know what to do. But as long as your intentions are honest you can't go wrong. Each person has to come to terms with their own challenges and learn to find their own happiness inside themselves, whatever their situation.

Let yourself off the unhappy hook

We really can give ourselves a hard time, can't we? As soon as we begin to work on changing our negative thinking patterns we immediately notice something quite surprising. It seems that we have a voice inside us that is continually faultfinding and bringing us down. In psychology this voice is known as the 'inner critic' and it is widely recognised as one of the greatest inhibitors of a happy state of mind. It is the voice that agrees with us when we doubt ourselves; it says, 'Yes you are not good enough.' It reminds us of our weaknesses and past failures, and when we are about to take an assertive step it will question our right to do so with such comments as 'Just who do you think you are?' The inner critic is also very good at below the belt tactics; it knows our weak spots and works on our guilt by questioning what we 'should' be doing and what we 'ought' to be thinking.

There are two very important things to know about the inner critic: we all have one and it never stops criticising.

Once we know these things it gets very much easier to loosen its harmful grip. The refrains of the inner critic are a collection of condemnations and disapprovals that we heard at a young age and which we are still hanging on to for some reason. The reason is usually simply that we have never before become aware of this recital of negativity. But as soon as we start to listen for our inner critical voice we hear it all the time. Its job is to criticise and it will keep on doing that (don't we just know it!) but we don't need to give it the time of day. Next time you hear yourself thinking or saying such things as: 'I always make mistakes'; 'I'm stupid'; 'It's out of my league'; 'I haven't got a chance'; 'I always mess up', you are listening to your inner critic. As soon as you recognise its negative tone take the following action:

- Hear what it is saying and then challenge it.
- Ask yourself if it's speaking the truth. For example, do you really always mess up? No, of course you don't, but if you believe this to be true you will immobilise yourself.
- Replace this critical thought with a positive affirmation. In the example given you could say 'I always do the very best I can.'

How to rephrase self-criticisms

Even if the inner critic was speaking a grain of truth, its harsh voice would not motivate us to make any useful changes. Psychologist Dr Albert Ellis coined this great phrase, 'Stop shoulding on yourself,' which explains how we put ourselves down by telling ourselves that we *should* be or act different in some way. In this way our inner critic scrambles our accurate views of whatever is going on and turns them into criticisms. Make a list of all the things that you think you should or shouldn't be doing; here are a few examples:

I should take more exercise.
I should be kinder to my sister.
I shouldn't make mistakes.
I should be more positive.
I shouldn't let things get me down.
I should be happier.
I shouldn't be grumpy.
I shouldn't eat that second piece of cake.

Well, perhaps I do need to take more exercise and I could be kinder to my sister, but shoulding relies on making us feel guilty and ashamed and this approach will never motivate positive change. Look at your own list and become aware of how you feel when you read out your items; it's enough to make you reach for a third slice of that cake, isn't it?

Shoulding doesn't help us to make happy new changes so why not drop this unhelpful habit and try a different and more positive approach? For example, instead of telling myself that 'I should be more positive' (makes me feel not good enough) I could replace it with, ' I am working towards being more positive' (encourages me to keep going). Try changing your should list around and notice how the guilt just melts away! Happy people let themselves (and others) off the hook.

CHANGE ONE THING

ABOUT THE WAY YOU SEE THE WORLD

HAPPY PEOPLE HAVE A SPECIAL WAY OF VIEWING THE WORLD; THEY PUT HAPPINESS FIRST BEFORE ANYTHING ELSE. THIS MEANS THAT THEY WON'T LET ANYTHING GET IN THE WAY OF THEIR HAPPINESS; THEY WON'T LET THINGS GET THEM DOWN. THEY KEEP UPBEAT AND POSITIVE IN THE FACE OF DIFFICULTIES AND THEY CAN ALWAYS FIND SOME SILVER THREADS IN ANY BLACK CLOUD.

- WHEN THINGS DON'T LOOK SO GOOD REMEMBER WHAT HAPPY PEOPLE DO; THEY DRAW ON THEIR POSITIVE ENERGY AND DON'T LET THEMSELVES FALL INTO DEPRESSION.

- FACE YOUR CHALLENGES HEAD ON; LOOK THEM IN THE EYE AND SEE THEM FOR WHAT THEY ARE.

- NOW CALL ON YOUR INNER RESERVES AND BE DETERMINED TO STAY POSITIVE.

- KNOW THAT EVERY SITUATION, HOWEVER BLEAK OR TRAUMATIC, WILL CONTAIN A SPARK OF BRIGHTNESS.

- CONGRATULATE YOURSELF FOR YOUR OPTIMISM IN THE FACE OF ADVERSITY AND LOOK FOR THAT SPARK OF POSITIVITY THAT IS ALWAYS SOMEWHERE TO BE FOUND IN THE NEGATIVE.

- JUST THE ACT OF LOOKING FOR THE SILVER LINING WILL HELP TO LIFT YOU OUT OF A LOW MOOD.

Happy people are motivated people

HAPPINESS → SELF-BELIEF → MOTIVATION → POSITIVE
ACTION → MORE HAPPINESS

UNHAPPINESS → INERTIA → DEMOTIVATION → INACTION
→ MORE UNHAPPINESS

A lack of desire to get up and go can lead to deep unhappiness. We can look around at all the things that need doing and allow ourselves to be overwhelmed by the prospect; everything might start to get us down. At this stage it's easy to put things off whilst we wait for a time when we will feel more motivated, but procrastination only increases our unhappiness. Waiting to get yourself motivated leads to increased self-doubt and lack of confidence because the longer we wait the more impossible it feels to do anything. How can we lift ourselves out of this cycle?

When I meet clients who are low on 'get up and go' I always question their self-talk. How are they treating themselves? Are they acting like their own best friend and giving themselves support and encouragement or are they tying themselves up in knots of self-criticism and self-doubt? Next time you find yourself locked in inertia check the nature of your self-talk.

The wonderful news is that as soon as we stop beating ourselves up (metaphorically speaking, that is) something rather amazing starts to happen; we begin to see exciting new possibilities on the horizon. As soon as we ditch the self-doubts and refuse to respond to the drone of our inner critic we are filled with self-belief and optimistic energy and anything feels possible. The greatest way to get motivated is to take action (the tiniest step will do). But in order to make that first move we must feel some of this vital and hopeful 'can-do' energy.

Whenever you feel demotivated you can easily break this spell by following this simple plan:

The get up and go action plan

Step 1 **Check your self-talk.** Are you bringing yourself down and lacking in confidence?

Step 2 **Ignore those inner criticisms** and recognise your real worth and ability.

Step 3 **Be your own best friend** and talk yourself up; of course you can do whatever it takes!

Step 4 **Take a realistic look at your 'to-do' list** and cross off all the things that you think you should or ought to do.

Step 5 **Choose one thing that you would love to do** and do it as soon as possible; you will feel greatly empowered and energised.

Step 6 **Act now** with your new-found optimism and tackle something that you have been putting off.

Step 7 **Congratulate yourself** for breaking out of a negative cycle.

And once you have done this and shown yourself how action can override low motivation you will have a foolproof plan that will get you going whenever you need it. You now know how to lift yourself out of that stuck, demotivated and unhappy cycle and into the cycle of motivation, positive action and increased happiness.

REFRESH AND RENEW

SEE YOUR THOUGHTS JUST FLY AWAY

WHEN YOUR MIND IS BUZZING WITH THOUGHTS AND PREOCCUPATIONS AND YOU ARE FEELING STRETCHED TRY THIS NEAT LITTLE VISUALISATION.

- SIT COMFORTABLY AND CLOSE YOUR EYES.

- BECOME AWARE OF THE BUZZING OF YOUR THOUGHTS AROUND YOUR HEAD.

- IMAGINE THAT EACH THOUGHT IS A BUMBLEBEE.

- NOW VISUALISE A HIVE FOR YOUR BEES AND WATCH AS EACH ONE BUZZES OFF AND ENTERS THE HIVE.

- WAIT UNTIL EVERY BEE HAS GONE AND THEN YOU WILL KNOW THAT YOUR MIND IS AT PEACE.

- STAY IN THIS CALM AND QUIET SPACE FOR AS LONG AS YOU WISH.

YOU CAN ALSO USE THIS TECHNIQUE DURING YOUR BUSY DAY. IF A MEETING GETS TOO MUCH JUST SEE YOUR BEES GOING TO THEIR HIVE AND KNOW THAT YOU ARE RELAXED AND FREE OF TENSION. OR YOU COULD USE IT AS YOU NEGOTIATE YOUR TROLLEY AROUND THE SUPERMARKET. WHEN YOUR THOUGHTS BUZZ OFF YOUR MIND CAN RELAX, AND YOUR BODY WILL FOLLOW YOUR MIND. LET GO AND CHILL!

Day 4 TODAY'S HAPPINESS ROUNDUP

Circle your happiness score and fill out the appropriate
sections in your journal to create your assessment of what
happened today.

MY HAPPINESS SCORE FOR THE DAY

TOTALLY   FABULOUS
FED-UP

1   2   3   4   5   6   7   8   9   10

Most significant event of the day

....

....

My main concern of the day

....

....

What can I do about this, if anything?

....

....

Most useful happiness strategies today

....

....

What went well today

....

....

Three things that made me smile today

....

....

Now add anything else that has been significant today.

Final reflections

- Those who describe themselves as 'very happy' are no more beautiful, sociable or successful than the average person.
- Finding happiness cannot be regarded as a competition. True happiness derives from raising the bar for yourself and not comparing yourself with other people.
- Unhappiness is not the beginning of the end, it is merely a sign that it's time to move on and make a new choice.
- When we stop beating ourselves up with self-criticism we open a door to hopeful feelings and positive, assertive action.
- Each time you rise above adversity and see the hidden opportunity in a dark cloud you become stronger and happier.

Day 5

Take the Right Path

The path of joy involves valuing yourself and monitoring where you put your time.

SANAYA ROMAN

Happiness is not in the mere possession of money; it lies in the joy of achievement, in the thrill of creative effort.

FRANKLIN D. ROOSEVELT

Would you be happier if you had more money? A quick straw poll amongst friends, colleagues and clients showed that 100 per cent believed that they would. We all know exactly what we would do if we had more cash, don't we; how could it not make us feel better? But repeated research demonstrates that money does not buy us happiness. In Britain, since 1950, income levels have increased threefold but happiness levels have remained the same, and it is estimated that 2 million of the population are now taking antidepressants.

James Montier, who is global equity strategist for investment bank Dresdner Kleinwort Wasserstein, has written a report called, 'It Doesn't Pay: Materialism and the Pursuit of Happiness'. He suggests that once we are earning £25,000 and upwards money becomes more and more irrelevant to genuine happiness. Although we could argue about whether there is actually a real financial cut-off point as he suggests, perhaps it is more useful to concentrate on his view that increased happiness comes from the value of our experiences rather than material possessions. He says: 'We have a bizarre idea of what we need. People very often talk about needing the latest fashionable clothes or needing the newest, trendiest technological toy, often exacerbated by an insistence on social comparisons, keeping up with the Joneses. But happiness should be an absolute concept not a relative one.'

Now you might well be thinking that this is a bit hard to take from a chap who is an investment banker and obviously not short of cash. And you might also be thinking that if you had a bit more money you could afford to indulge in more happy-making experiences. But he is making an important point because all the experts agree that unless you are in the bottom third of the economic pile, the extent of your wealth will have *no bearing on the state of your happiness.*

Dr Raj Persaud says that one of the laws of human behaviour is that we gradually get used to the good things that increase our wellbeing (we habituate to them) and so our happiness levels start to fall as we begin to take our new positive changes for granted so that: 'Profound improvements in technology, organisation and wealth in a society therefore seldom return the same scale of transformation in well-being in the population. This is referred to in the psychology of happiness as getting trapped on a hedonic treadmill, no matter how fast you run – no matter how much you get, you still want more.'

Yes, we are all acquainted with the desire to consume and we know how addictive it can be; just how many handbags do we really need? (And speaking of bags, did you know that British women spent an astounding £350 million on them in 2005?) Well, I love the good things in life as much as the next girl but I think we all know that more wine, chocolate, shoes, MP3 players and the rest can never deliver lasting happiness and fulfilment.

The three paths to happiness

Professor Martin Seligman suggests that there are three paths to happiness: the pleasant life, the good life and the meaningful life.

The pleasant life refers to what we probably think of when considering whether we are happy from moment to moment (e.g. a glass of wine, trip to the shops, watching *EastEnders*). The good life comes from our creative engagement in our work, hobbies, family and other relationships or any activity that we find rewarding and challenging. And finally the meaningful life, which Seligman considers the most underrated of all. This path requires us to use our personal strengths and abilities for a purpose greater than our own (e.g. volunteering, politics, community action).

In a now classic exercise that Seligman calls 'Philanthropy versus Fun', his psychology students engaged in one philanthropic activity and one pleasurable activity and then wrote about their experiences. He claimed that the results were 'life-changing' and that the afterglow of the fun activity (eating ice cream, watching a film) paled in comparison with the effects of the kind action (helping at the school fair, volunteering at a soup kitchen). The reason, Seligman proposes, is that kindness is a gratification: 'It calls on your strengths to rise to an occasion and meet a challenge. Kindness is not accompanied by a separate stream of positive emotion, like joy; rather it consists in total engagement and in the loss of self-consciousness.'

It appears that the route to long-lasting happiness leads us away from the shopping mall and into an investigation of the degree to which we feel that we are really engaged with our lives.

CHANGE ONE THING

BY FOCUSING ON WHAT REALLY BRINGS YOU JOY AND SATISFACTION

CHECK OUT HOW THESE THREE PATHS TO HAPPINESS SHOW UP IN YOUR LIFE. TAKE ONE AT A TIME AND REFLECT ON THEIR MEANING TO YOU.

THE PLEASANT LIFE

NAME THE MOMENT-TO-MOMENT ACTIVITIES THAT GIVE YOU PLEASURE IN THE SHORT TERM. FOR EXAMPLE, GOING OUT TO DINNER; PLAYING COMPUTER GAMES; GOING TO THE PUB; READING A NOVEL.

REFLECT UPON HOW DOING EACH OF THESE THINGS LIFTS YOUR MOOD AND MAKES YOU FEEL GOOD FOR A WHILE.

THE GOOD LIFE

NAME ALL THOSE ACTIVITIES WHICH CALL ON YOUR CREATIVE ENERGY AND ARE MORE CHALLENGING AND THEREFORE MORE REWARDING. FOR EXAMPLE, PLAYING BADMINTON; HAVING A FAMILY BARBECUE; WRITING A REPORT FOR WORK; DIY; PLAYING THE PIANO; MAKING A BIRTHDAY CAKE.

AGAIN CONSIDER THE EFFECTS THAT THESE ACTIONS HAVE ON YOUR MOOD AND NOTICE THAT YOUR SATISFACTION LEVELS RISE ACCORDING TO THE AMOUNT OF PERSONAL ENERGY AND COMMITMENT THAT YOU INVEST IN THE PROJECT.

Finding your purpose

Some people seem to have an obvious path ahead of them: they know what they love to do; they are clearly focused career wise and maybe they are even in a great relationship. But although they might look as though they have got it made, you can be quite sure that they have had to carve out these happy outcomes for themselves and they have to keep working on them to maintain them. Our lives are creative endeavours; we bring our energy, hopes, beliefs and expectations into the arena and make them what we will.

You are unique, amazing and wonderful and you came here for a purpose. And when you are engaged in activities that match your strengths and talents then you will feel this sense of purpose flowing through you and your life will feel meaningful and happy.

When clients come for coaching they are often looking for that inner spark of creative energy that will get them back on track again. We all lose direction at times and when this happens we feel as though we are not getting the most from life; and we are not! Some clients actually say that they feel as if they are on the wrong path. When someone describes their life in this way I usually take them back to basics and we look at how they can get back on track again. I find that people have often forgotten what they are good at and are not using their unique creativity in a way that satisfies their soul; if you are feeling like a square peg in a round hole then you will know what this means.

10 ways to get back on track

1   **Pursue your passions.** Do more of what you love to do. Act when you feel that 'get up and go' energy coursing through you. I am always telling clients that they will only achieve their goals if they are mad about them and this is so true. We are usually attracted to a course of action which draws on our skills, so begin to notice what attracts you and develop this.

2   **Notice where your energy flags and you lose interest.** If you are bored by a prospective project it usually means that you are not going to give it your all. Ask yourself if this course of action suits you. Are you doing this because you think you ought to or because someone else expects you to?

3   **Follow your instincts.** Don't just deliberate and evaluate. Start to check into your gut feelings. What does your instinct tell you to do? What feels good? Use your head and your heart to come to a decision and when you just *know* something is right then follow that knowledge.

4   **Make a list of your skills and strengths.** Name your talents; get them down in black and white. What are you good at? Brainstorm and create a list of your unique personal qualities.

5   **Act with discrimination.** When you feel that you are just putting in time then it is a sign that you are running way below your potential. If you feel like this in any area of your life begin to question your motives. Why are you doing whatever you are doing? What action would you prefer to be taking?

6   **Be ready to make changes.** If you are feeling like the proverbial square peg then it's time to find a new niche that fits you. Change can be unsettling but if you decide to welcome it then it can feel liberating! Approach potential life transformations with a pioneer spirit and let the excitement of the new carry you through.

7   **Stay open and aware.** You never know what might be around the next corner. Adopt a hopefully expectant response and you will attract exciting new outcomes. Stay in the positive zone and remember that anything is possible!

8   **Tap into your creative energy.** When you lose yourself in a task you are reaching creative heights as you become totally engaged and lose any sense of self-consciousness. Ask yourself when this happens for you. What does this insight tell you about yourself?

9 **Make a commitment.** As soon as your heart and mind know what you need to do to bring the oomph back into your life then you must commit wholeheartedly to following this through. Nothing less than 100 per cent commitment will do. Take that first step towards activating your plan and you are on your way.

10 **Trust.** Trust yourself, your dreams and the universe. There are no lucky breaks; you make your own luck. There are no coincidences, you attract the circumstances you need to realise your goals. Believe that you will fulfil your purpose and you will!

H A P P I N E S S   T I P

STOP, SIMPLIFY AND APPRECIATE

WE ARE OFTEN SO BUSY KEEPING UP WITH OURSELVES THAT WE FORGET THE MIRACULOUS WONDER OF JUST BEING ALIVE. TAKE A MOMENT TO STOP, TO SIMPLIFY AND TO APPRECIATE AND YOU WILL FEEL REJUVENATED.

- FOCUS ON WHAT YOU HAVE RATHER THAN ON WHAT YOU DON'T HAVE.

- LOVE THE SKIN YOU ARE IN AND VALUE YOUR BODY AND ALL IT DOES FOR YOU.

- GIVE THANKS FOR THE FOOD ON YOUR TABLE.

- VALUE YOUR FRIENDSHIPS.

- CHERISH YOUR LOVED ONES.

- BE GLAD TO BE ALIVE.

- LOOK FOR THE BEAUTY IN YOUR LIFE AND YOUR LIFE
  WILL BECOME A BEAUTIFUL EXPERIENCE.

Doing what makes you happy

When someone tells me how they find it hard to accomplish an objective my first question to them is always, 'How much do you want your goal?' People who are madly passionate about whatever they are chasing have supreme can-do energy and won't take no for an answer; they are highly motivated because they are pursuing a goal that makes them feel happy. When we are less than 100 per cent engaged in our outcomes we invite ourselves to fail.

Supermodel Heidi Klum says: 'I am a go-getter. There is always more than one way to do things. If someone says no, it doesn't necessarily mean no. But you have to be inventive.' Go-getters find creative ways to resolve setbacks because they are totally committed to achieving their goal; they know what they want and they are only too happy to go for it. If you have been struggling to achieve something and it just doesn't seem to be coming together ask yourself how much you want a result. Sometimes we can find ourselves continually failing to achieve because we are trying to do something that doesn't really suit us.

Leah's story

Leah 20, was studying to be a pharmacist at a London university. She contacted me just before she was to sit her second year exams because she said she was beginning to feel very negative and was finding it hard to concentrate on revision. She told me that she had been a grade A student throughout her school career and had won the school prize for science after the A-level results came out. Her parents were incredibly proud of her achievements, particularly as she was the first person in the family to get to university. But when she got there Leah began to lose interest in her subjects and became fascinated by psychology. She had friends in the department and began reading their books. As the first year progressed she felt less and less motivated by her course and fell behind with her work. She didn't want to tell her parents the truth and so she pretended that all was well. She said, 'I so didn't want to let them down.'

After a couple of sessions with me Leah realised that what she really wanted to do was to switch courses and study psychology but she was afraid of her parents' reaction. In the end she faced her feelings and went home one weekend to tell them. They were concerned at first but they did understand and Leah changed her course.

I meet many people who are on a path they no longer wish to take. Some like Leah train for a certain profession only to discover years later that it doesn't make them happy. Others are in a relationship which no longer works. If your motivation levels are low then check that the goals you seek are making you happy. Happy people are creatively engaged because they love their goals.

ACTIVITY: KNOWING WHAT I WANT

- MAKE A LIST OF YOUR CURRENT GOALS.

EXAMPLE: LEARN SPANISH

PAY OFF MY CREDIT CARD DEBTS

LOSE WEIGHT

SPEND MORE TIME WITH THE CHILDREN

- GIVE EACH ONE A SCORE FROM 1 TO 10.

1 = YOU FEEL A COMPLETE LACK OF INTEREST

10 = YOU ARE TOTALLY MOTIVATED

EXAMPLE: LEARN SPANISH   4

PAY OFF MY CREDIT CARD DEBTS   10

LOSE WEIGHT   9

SPEND MORE TIME WITH THE CHILDREN 10

IT IS NEVER WORTH PURSUING ANY GOAL THAT DOES NOT SCORE 10 IN THIS EXERCISE. 9 IS NOT ENOUGH, IT ALLOWS AN ESCAPE ROUTE BECAUSE IT DOES NOT ENGAGE TOTAL COMMITMENT. THE TWO GOALS IN THE EXAMPLE THAT SCORE 10 HAVE THE ONLY CHANCE OF SUCCESS.

NEVER WASTE YOUR TIME WITH FANCIFUL PLANS THAT YOU KNOW WILL EVENTUALLY COME TO NOTHING. EACH TIME YOU SAY THAT YOU WILL DO SOMETHING AND YOU DON'T DO IT, YOU WILL INCREASE YOUR FEELINGS OF LACK OF SELF-RESPECT AND THIS WILL LEAD TO UNHAPPINESS.

USE THIS TECHNIQUE WHENEVER YOU WANT TO TEST HOW MUCH YOU REALLY WANT TO ACHIEVE A GOAL.

Know your strengths

As a nation we British are notoriously bad at blowing our own trumpets, aren't we? We admire self-deprecation and deplore self-satisfaction but this cultural habit might not be so good for bringing joy to our hearts.

When we refer back to Seligman's three paths to happiness we see that the good life and the meaningful life largely depend upon the use of our creative energy, our talents and our strengths. But how can we know what we are good at if we are continually hiding our light?

Many years ago when I lived in Cornwall I ran a pilot project for the Employment Service. My brief was to give career guidance to unemployed 18–24 year olds. The month course included CV writing and interview skills but I soon discovered that the most important part of the job was getting these young people to value exactly what they did have to offer. Feeling unemployable is a self-esteem buster that just reinforces low self-worth (how can I be of any use to anyone when no one values me enough to give me a decent job?). On the first day of a new course I would give the participants a handout which simply asked them to list their skills and strengths. It might sound a simple enough task but it always caused havoc. Sometimes it took three weeks of motivation and encouragement before all the group members could fill out this form. I often spent days trying to convince some of them that they had *anything* to offer, and in the end, of course, their employment success completely depended on them being able to value themselves. If applicants don't think that they are good enough to get the job then they certainly won't convince an employer to engage them.

I learned such a lot about the power of self-belief (and the inhibiting power of the lack of it) when I ran these courses. Young, fit people would stand up in that training room and try to convince me and the rest of the group that they hadn't got anything they could write on their skills and strengths form; it was a bit like an AA meeting sometimes! But by the end of the month most of them would be able to give a presentation of their skills to the group, they would have written a CV and some would even be about to go on interview. These miracles occurred because the unemployed youngsters saw a reflection of themselves in the rest of the group. As I bullied and cajoled in an effort to keep up the motivation levels most of these young people rose to the occasion. When one member was defeated and gloomy another would remind him of what he was offering to the group and in the end it was this communal motivation that brought about the good results.

But let's go back to the original key issue that opened all the wounds: the skills and strengths handout. Try this yourself now. Brainstorm all the things that you do well and don't be a shrinking violet! Think creatively about this, it is not just a list of academic achievements, artistic talents or sporting prowess. Consider your personal qualities and if this is hard ask a friend to tell you what you are good at; you will be amazed by what you hear! You might be a good organiser, a clear thinker, a trustworthy friend. Maybe you love learning new things or are always ready to take a risk. Others might admire your integrity and discretion, your listening skills or your ability to get people moving. Think laterally about this task and write down anything and everything you can think of. What a list!

We are at our happiest when we are tapping into those things that we do the best. Have another look at your list and consider if you are using your talents and abilities to the full.

Are you maximising your potential? If you are, you will feel suitably challenged but equally rewarded and satisfied, and if you are not you will feel undervalued, unappreciated, dissatisfied and unhappy.

Why philanthropy is fun

A recent article in the *Mail on Sunday*'s *You* magazine was called 'Meet the A-list Philanthropists'. Charlotte Methven, who wrote the piece, suggests that altruism is flourishing more than ever in our supposedly materialistic age. She says: 'Even high-living celebrity Tara Palmer-Tomkinson shows her more generous side by cooking meals and soup and handing out cash to homeless people. Last December she even paid for a beggar to spend the night in a Kensington hotel. Today's do-gooders aren't just hosting cocktail parties or throwing money at worthy causes; they don't simply wear rubber wristbands or red Aids ribbons; nor do they stick to the safe confines of giving to the arts. These women are out there in the field, getting their hands dirty. . . . They juggle motherhood and careers with charitable endeavours, sacrificing their most precious commodity – time – for the greater good. Many have been born into privilege or have made a lot of money – or both – and feel the need to "give something back".' This sentiment fits exactly with the description of the 'meaningful life'; which is one that connects us with a bigger purpose and brings a feeling of total engagement.

Volunteering in a good cause brings as much happiness as doubling our income and such volunteers also increase their life expectancy. A study at Vanderbilt University in Tennessee showed that whilst happy people were more likely to engage in voluntary work they also became even happier, the more they volunteered. Numerous studies show that when we feel good we are more likely to pass on our feeling to others in acts of kindness. Psychologists call this the 'feel-good, do-good phenomenon'. Yes, happiness just creates more and more happiness!

Angelina Jolie is a United Nations Goodwill Ambassador and she says, 'I've learnt that it actually does feel better to give than to receive. I think I'm finally on track with what I should be doing with my life.' And Jemima Khan, Sir James Goldsmith's daughter, echoes this response when she says, 'Life is utterly pointless unless you have a purpose that you believe in. It shapes your life and gives you self-respect.' Jemima was an indomitable fundraiser when she lived in Pakistan and was married to philanthropist Imran Khan. Now living in London she is a UK ambassador for Unicef. Many other famous women, including Elle Macpherson, Stella McCartney and J. K. Rowling are treading a similar path with a practical, hands-on approach to volunteering.

Ok, so we might not have the same resources as these women, but the message is clear: if we want to live a meaningful life we must do something that is meaningful.

CHANGE ONE THING

SPREAD YOUR HAPPINESS ABOUT

NEGATIVE VIBES SPREAD LIKE WILDFIRE, BUT THEN AGAIN SO DO POSITIVE ONES. NEXT TIME YOU ARE FEELING GOOD REMEMBER THAT WHAT YOU ARE EXPERIENCING IS PART OF A GIANT WAVE OF HAPPINESS, WHICH CAN SPREAD TO ENCOMPASS ALL THE PEOPLE WHO YOU COME IN CONTACT WITH.

There is a lovely J. M. Barrie quote where he says: 'Those who bring sunshine into the lives of others cannot keep it from themselves.' Try this today:

- At your next feel-good moment, imagine that you are surfing a giant wave of happiness.

- Feel the positive momentum drawing you on and lifting your spirits.

- Look around you wherever you are and imagine that everyone in your vicinity is able to leap up on to this wave.

- Imagine this as you are talking to a colleague in the office or you are passing a stranger on the street; see these people surfing the happiness wave and spreading their own good feelings about.

- Bring others into your sunshine and you will feel even happier.

The positive approach to unhappiness

It is quite natural and normal to experience unhappy times. No one lives in a perpetual state of bliss. And being positive doesn't mean that we say that things are fine when they are obviously not or that we have to wear rose-tinted glasses or be smiling all the time. A positive person is a realist; she is hopefully expectant and trusts in the benevolence of the universe but she also knows that bad things do happen and that they are an inevitable part of life.

We want to be happy and feel optimistic because this attitude brings out the best in us and in others, but we also need to be able to allow ourselves to be unhappy at times. The positive approach to unhappiness is a 5-step contingency plan for you to fall back on when times get rough:

Step 1 Become aware of your feelings by taking an emotional step back so that you don't become totally engulfed.

Step 2 Remind yourself that these emotions will pass.

Step 3 Now you can allow yourself to really get in touch with your feelings. Know that you can only let go of an emotion once you have felt it all the way through.

Step 4 When the intensity is passed and the heat is off you will feel different. Stay with these new feelings and let them be, don't try to change them.

Step 5 Step 4 inevitably leads to Step 5. Once you can live with your feelings you will naturally begin to let them go.

We are often afraid of our feelings, imagining that they will cause us terrible emotional pain but actually it is the denial of feelings that causes our misery. So if something happens that sets us back and we deny how we feel (because we are afraid of our reaction) then we will create double the unhappiness.

Our emotional states are always just 'passing through'; they come and go according to our whims and fancies and what can hurt us one day might go unnoticed the next. I find it a great comfort to know that I have only to let my emotions do their own thing for a while and that then they will change and move on. A contingency plan is always a great fallback position in any circumstances; it offers support and an element of control. Next time unhappiness falls upon you try using this approach and observe your feelings passing through you as you simply let them go.

REFRESH AND RENEW

THE TRANQUIL LAKE

RELAX AND CLOSE YOUR EYES.

- IMAGINE A CALM LAKE AHEAD OF YOU.

- BEND DOWN AND CHOOSE A SMOOTH PEBBLE FROM THE STONES AROUND THE EDGE OF THE WATER. FEEL THE STONE IN YOUR HAND AND LET IT REPRESENT ANY DIFFICULTY THAT YOU ARE EXPERIENCING.

- NOW THROW THE PEBBLE AS FAR AS YOU CAN INTO THE LAKE. WATCH THE RIPPLES FORM IN CONCENTRIC CIRCLES ACROSS THE SURFACE.

- AS YOU WATCH THE RIPPLES FORM AND DISAPPEAR IMAGINE THAT THEY REPRESENT ALL THE EMOTIONS THAT YOU HAVE TIED UP IN THIS PARTICULAR EXPERIENCE.

- FEEL THE EMOTIONS POURING THROUGH YOU AS YOU WATCH THE RIPPLES ON THE WATER.

- AND THEN, WHEN THE SURFACE IS CALM ONCE MORE, FEEL THAT YOU TOO ARE NOW CALM AND STILL AND THAT YOU HAVE RELEASED ALL YOUR DIFFICULT FEELINGS.

- AS YOU LOOK AT THE STILL CALM SURFACE OF THIS BEAUTIFUL LAKE YOU KNOW THAT YOU TOO ARE CALM AND STILL AND RELAXED.

Day 5 TODAY'S HAPPINESS ROUNDUP

Again it's time to reflect on your day. Circle your score and fill out the sections in your journal.

MY HAPPINESS SCORE FOR THE DAY

TOTALLY   FABULOUS
FED-UP
1   2   3   4   5   6   7   8   9   10

Most significant event of the day

....

....

My main concern of the day

....

....

What can I do about this, if anything?

....

....

Most useful happiness strategies today

....

....

What went well today

....

....

Three things that made me smile today

....

....

Now add anything else that has been significant today.

Final reflections

- No matter how fast we run, no matter how much we get, we still want more.
- Our levels of satisfaction rise according to the amount of personal energy and commitment we invest in a project.
- Happy people love their goals.
- Whenever we are less than 100 per cent engaged in our outcomes we invite ourselves to fail.
- Bring others into your sunshine and you will feel even happier.

Day 6

Things are Definitely Looking Up

In letting go of wanting something special to occur, maybe we can realise that something special is already occurring, and is always occurring.

JON KABAT-ZINN

Look to this Day! . . .
For Yesterday is but a Dream,
And Tomorrow is only a Vision;
But Today well lived makes
Every Yesterday a Dream of Happiness,
And every Tomorrow a Vision of Hope.

KALIDASA

I love this passage because it reminds us that we can only find happiness when we stop and appreciate this very moment; only then can we feel the true power of Now! It's only too easy for us to take our fabulous world for granted, but whenever we begin to do this we lose our sense of wonder and this can eventually lead to a loss of happiness and hope.

Today begins with the affirmation that 'Things are definitely looking up', which of course is a great mood motivator and also a reminder that our decision to be happy directly affects the way that we feel. Benjamin Franklin put this another way when he said, 'To the discontented man no chair is easy.' Well, some chairs are certainly more uncomfortable than others but the person who chooses optimism over pessimism and appreciation over complaint will always find it easier to deal with lumpy upholstery and broken springs. However, there is an even greater benefit for those of us who are lifting our energy and working on increasing our positivity; this attitude gives us the enthusiasm and vigour to make changes so that we can choose to sit in new chairs if we wish.

Happiness and contentment are revitalising and rejuvenating whilst misery and discontent are ageing and debilitating. Charles Dickens thought this subject worth commenting upon, saying, 'Cheerfulness and contentment are great beautifiers, and are famous preservers of youthful looks.' When you smile you radiate positive energy and studies show that a smiling person is perceived as being more attractive, sincere, sociable and competent than a non-smiling person. Happy people are more at ease with themselves and this look inspires the confidence of others, so get smiling and you will quickly notice the difference in the way that others react. We all need smiles because we thrive on happiness and on sharing our good feelings with others. Mother Teresa gave us a great reminder to keep smiling when she said, 'Every time you smile at someone, it is an action of love, a gift to that person, a beautiful thing.' Share your gifts and your happiness and all the good vibes will be reflected back to you, which will further increase your happiness levels.

CHANGE ONE THING

BY INCREASING YOUR SMILES PER HOUR

- EVEN A FAKE SMILE WILL MAKE US FEEL HAPPIER, SO ON A GREY DAY JUST 'FAKE IT UNTIL YOU MAKE IT' AS THE SAYING GOES. ACTUALLY THIS REALLY DOES WORK. SLAP ON A GRIN EVEN WHEN YOU DON'T FEEL IN THE MOOD AND THEN JUST WAIT FOR THAT FEEL-GOOD CHEMICAL LIFT. TRY THIS NOW; IT'S SUCH A SIMPLE AND EFFECTIVE TECHNIQUE.

- GET INTO THE HABIT OF SMILING MORE. FOCUS ON THE EFFECT THAT YOUR SMILE HAS ON OTHERS. SMILE AT PEOPLE WHO LOOK MISERABLE. GIVE OTHERS THIS GIFT OF HAPPINESS AND NOTICE THEIR REACTION.

- THE MORE YOU REMEMBER TO SMILE THE EASIER IT GETS. ONE SMILE LEADS TO ANOTHER AND ANOTHER . . .

- BECOME A SMILEY PERSON AND OTHERS WILL BE ATTRACTED TO YOUR ENERGY. RESEARCH SHOWS THAT PEOPLE ARE MORE LIKELY TO SPEAK TO SOMEONE WHO HAS SMILED AT THEM (NATURALLY!).

- AND DON'T FORGET THAT SMILING IS A VERY EFFECTIVE FACELIFT!

- CHECK IN TO YOUR FACIAL EXPRESSION WHENEVER YOU REMEMBER AND PUT ON A SMILE AND YOU WILL FEEL FABULOUS!

Progress review

You are now halfway through the programme and so this is the perfect time to take stock and evaluate your progress. How good have you become at adopting the happiness habit? Are you feeling more positive about life than you did when you started on Day 1? What makes you feel good about yourself? Are there any specific situations where you find your happiness levels dropping? What are you learning about the ways that you deal with the world? Take a look at your journal entries and in particular at your daily happiness roundups and notice if any patterns are emerging. Which techniques and strategies are working best? How can you incorporate these into your daily life? Where do your difficulties lie? Are there certain issues that cause you to doubt yourself? Are there certain people who affect your optimistic spirit? In other words, what brings you down and why? Look back at the cycle of unhappiness and cycle of happiness diagrams on pages 21 and 22 in Day 1, and reflect upon what happens to you when you go from one cycle to the other.

What forces you out of the happiness zone and into the cycle of unhappiness?

. . . .

Where do you lose your self-confidence and why?

. . . .

What does it take to lift you back into the cycle of happiness; how do you raise your spirits?

. . . .

What does happiness mean to you?

. . . .

Which self-beliefs endanger your happiness?

. . . .

Describe the way you behave when you are feeling happy.

. . . .

Which of the happiness strategies that you have used so far
have been the most effective?

. . . .

What is the single most important thing that you could do to
increase your happiness levels at the moment?

. . . .

HAPPINESS TIP

ACCEPT YOURSELF JUST AS YOU ARE

IT'S GREAT TO HAVE HIGH SELF-EXPECTATIONS AND TO GO
FOR OUR GOALS BUT JUST MAKE SURE THAT YOU ARE NOT
SHOWING PERFECTIONIST TENDENCIES. THERE IS A THIN
LINE BETWEEN REACHING FOR OUR BEST AND HAVING
UNREALISTIC EXPECTATIONS OF WHAT WE CAN ACHIEVE.
PERFECTIONISTS ARE ALWAYS UNHAPPY BECAUSE THEY CAN
NEVER MEET THEIR OWN EXACTING STANDARDS; WHATEVER
THEY DO IS NEVER QUITE 'GOOD ENOUGH' AND SO THEY
ARE NOT ABLE TO RECOGNISE SUCCESS. IF WE CAN ONLY
SETTLE FOR PERFECTION THEN WE CAN NEVER ACTUALLY
COMPLETE A PROJECT OR BE SATISFIED WITH A

RELATIONSHIP OR EVEN ENJOY DAY-TO-DAY LIVING. PERFECTIONISTS ARE ALSO VERY CRITICAL OF THE SEEMING 'IMPERFECTIONS' OF OTHERS AND SO THEY FIND IT HARD TO MAKE AND KEEP FRIENDS. IF YOU EVER FIND YOURSELF STRIVING FOR THE ABSOLUTE AND THE UTTERLY IMPOSSIBLE JUST STOP AND REMIND YOURSELF THAT YOU ARE ONLY HUMAN.

- IF YOU CAN NEVER GET THAT PIECE OF WORK 'JUST RIGHT' YOU WILL NEVER FINISH IT. GIVE YOURSELF A REALISTIC DEADLINE AND GIVE IT YOUR BEST SHOT; THIS IS THE BEST THAT YOU CAN DO AND IT IS ENOUGH.

- IF YOU ARE STRUGGLING WITH CONFIDENCE ISSUES THEN YOU WILL NEVER BE SATISFIED WITH HOW YOU ARE. STOP COMPARING YOURSELF WITH AN UNREALISTIC IDEALISTIC SELF-IMAGE AND BEGIN TO LOVE WHO YOU REALLY ARE. NONE OF US IS PERFECT.

- DON'T EXPECT OTHERS TO NEVER MAKE MISTAKES; THEY WILL AND SO WILL YOU. GIVE THEM AND YOURSELF A BREAK AND LIFE WILL BECOME A MUCH MORE LIGHT-HEARTED AFFAIR.

Is something holding you back from happiness?

Each of us has unique strengths and talents and we are also uniquely challenged. What is hard for one is easy for another and vice versa. Do any of the following issues stand in the way of your happiness?

Are you:

Lacking in self-belief?

This will always undermine you and stop you feeling happy. If you can't demonstrate inner conviction then you will lose your self-respect and this leads into a deeply negative place. Focusing on your insecurities only makes them seem bigger and more important.

What to do Tackle your negative beliefs head on. Simply stop taking any notice of that self-critical voice that is always telling you that you are not good enough in some way. You *are* good enough! Remind yourself that you always do your best and that it is quite acceptable for you to make mistakes.

Acting like a victim?

It's so easy to fall into this trap when things are not going so well. We are all inclined to look for someone or something to blame when we are challenged. But this tactic never works. If we lay the blame for our misfortune on anything or anyone then we give away all the power we have to make the situation good. For example, if 'he is to blame' then I must wait for him to change his behaviour, or, if the circumstances are at fault, then I must wait for them to change. And if the rain is to blame, well who knows how long I might have to wait?

What to do Accept responsibility for whatever is going on in your life. Yes, others make mistakes and can affect us badly but we have the power to change our lives and this feeling of control is vital to our happiness. Stop any blaming activity and seek ways to improve your situation. Decide not to let yourself be victimised by anyone or anything: walk away if necessary, or wait patiently until a more auspicious time or buy an umbrella! Do whatever it takes to take charge of your life.

Feeling shy and self-conscious?

Is it hard to step forward into your own spotlight? Are you hanging about in the shadows watching others do what you want to do and have what you want to have? If you are in the habit of shrinking into the background you will always feel like an underachiever and this is guaranteed to take away life's sparkle.

What to do Realise that you will never be happy until you can take the lead role in your life. When shyness beckons turn your attention away from your perceived shortcomings and focus on someone else. Look around for others who are lacking in confidence and give them a boost. You will soon forget all about yourself.

Shyness is linked with feelings of not being good enough so fight back with positive affirmations and assertive action. Take that risky step and you will feel like a new person. Happy people are always ready to take a chance because who knows what golden opportunities might be around the next corner?

Having difficulties with intimate relationships?

Do you find it difficult to stay in a long-term relationship? Is it hard to make good decisions about prospective partners? Are you in an unhealthy relationship (i.e. one that is not good for you?). Do you have difficulty in communicating your needs? Are you afraid that you might lose control in an intimate relationship? If you are struggling with relationship issues then join the majority who would also love to be in a happy and fulfilling partnership.

What to do Recognise that you attract the sort of relationship that you think you deserve. If you believe in yourself then others will be drawn to your aura of confidence and if you are self-critical then you will attract partners who will criticise you. Women are often keen to change a man in order to create the perfect relationship but as we all know this method never works. You can only alter a relationship by changing the way you are. So start to work on the relationship you are having with yourself; when that one is happy you will find it easier to have a happy relationship with someone else.

Lacking body confidence?

In a major survey of 5,000 women, 90 per cent said that they were 'depressed' by the appearance of their body, and one in ten admitted to being on a 'constant diet'. I think that these figures are actually quite conservative; most women have a poor self-image and this cuts into their happiness in a profound way.

What to do Stop comparing yourself with others and in particular with those gorgeous, perfect, airbrushed girls in glossy magazines. Love your body and what it does for you and appreciate your unique features. And if you are feeling depressed about your looks at the moment just get over yourself. You will never ever be happy if you are constantly obsessing about your appearance. Who do you think is looking at you and judging you in such a superficial way? Remember what matters most in your life and get a grip on what is really important. Did you choose your best friend because of her beauty? No, of course not, you care for her because of her inner qualities. It might help you to remember that it is unlikely that anyone is judging you because they are far too busy worrying about themselves!

Unable to make decisions?

Sometimes it is hard to know which route to take and we might start asking around for other people's opinions. It's fine to get feedback but in the end whatever you decide is down to you. If you are struggling with getting the clarity you need in order that you can make a good choice, just try the following technique.

What to do Discover your intention by asking this question: 'What do I want to happen?' Be clear and specific. Now consider the steps that you must take to reach your goal. Take the first step and the next step will become obvious. Trust your decision-making process and trust your own judgement and the more you do this the happier you will feel.

ACTIVITY: DO SOMETHING DIFFERENT

IF LIFE FEELS A BIT DULL THEN CHANGE YOUR USUAL HABITS. TURN OFF THE TELEVISION TONIGHT AND DO SOMETHING UNUSUAL.

- IF YOU ARE NOT ALONE WHY NOT PLAY A BOARD GAME OR CARDS?

- DO THE CROSSWORD IN THE PAPER.

- START READING THAT NEW NOVEL.

- MAKE A LOAF OF BREAD, A CAKE OR BISCUITS.

- LISTEN TO THE RADIO.

- PHONE SOMEONE YOU LOVE.

- TURN ON YOUR FAVOURITE MUSIC.

- GO OUT TO AN UNFAMILIAR PUB OR RESTAURANT.

DO SOMETHING DIFFERENT AND YOU WILL FEEL ENERGISED AND REVITALISED.

Choosing hope

The difference between a pessimist and an optimist lies in their relationship with hope. My dictionary defines hope as 'a feeling of desire for something and confidence in the possibility of its fulfilment'.

When we think that a situation is hopeless we lose strength, determination and happiness and when we are hopeful we are filled with enthusiasm and purpose. At challenging times we are obviously more inclined to negativity and it is just at these times that we most need a dose of hopefulness to see us through. Dr Tim Elliott, an expert in rehabilitation psychology, led a study testing the effects of hopefulness on a group of people who were paralysed by spinal cord injury. As time passed, the ones who were the most full of hope were less depressed and more mobile than the others.

Christopher Reeve battled courageously and hopefully in the face of his own paralysis and worked as an ambassador for all those struck down with spinal cord injuries. He said, 'When the unthinkable happens, the lighthouse is hope.

Once we choose hope, everything is possible.' Christopher Reeve reminds us that hope is a choice.

Violet's story

When I worked as a counsellor for CRUSE, the bereavement-counselling organisation, I met Violet who was in her late sixties. Her husband had died some months before and she was devastated. They had done everything together for the last forty years and they hadn't had any children. Violet said that she didn't know how she could possibly go on without Dan, who she called her 'best mate'.

When we lose someone close there is a natural grieving process that occurs and this can last for any length of time. I visited Violet for about six months and in that time I watched an amazing transformation occur. At the start there were many emotions that she wanted to discuss and she could go from depression to anger to denial to acceptance and back again many times during one visit. But as the months passed her sadness began to lift and then one day when I called she was full of excitement. She said that she had read about a volunteer scheme in the local paper which was asking for 'foster grandparents' to spend time with seriously ill children. At that visit she had fresh hope in her heart as we filled out her application form, and once Violet started on the scheme she didn't need me to call any more. At our final meeting she told me all about a six-year-old girl who she was teaching to knit and a teenage boy who she helped to make model aeroplanes. With this new energy Violet was finally able to clear out Dan's clothes, which she had thought that she would never be able to do. Of course she still missed him but she said that being with the children made her feel closer to Dan and that she now felt that he was still with her in some important way.

Hope is a choice that we make when we are ready to engage fully with our lives. Sometimes circumstances can knock us back and we have to wait a while before we can enjoy the pleasures of life again. But as soon as we are ready to look for it that spark of hopefulness is always there shining brightly.

CHANGE ONE THING

BECOME EVEN MORE DETERMINED

To embrace the habits of happiness and hopefulness we may need to call on our inner reserves of resilience, perseverance and determination.

Sometimes it is only too easy to give up and fall at the first hurdle but when we do this we let ourselves down and then we become downhearted.

- Never give up on yourself. Always do the very best job you can and be ready to give it *all* of your effort. This might mean carrying on even when you feel like giving up.

- Decide to be the sort of person who will always go that extra mile. As you become known for this personality trait you will attract many more positive opportunities, because people will know that they can rely on you and that you will always come through.

- Winners are people who always do the best they can. Because they are self-reliant they can never really lose even if things don't always work out

---

QUITE THE WAY THEY WISHED. WINNERS BOUNCE BACK AND THEY NEVER ADMIT DEFEAT. THIS COURAGEOUS ATTITUDE INCREASES THEIR FEELINGS OF OPTIMISM AND HOPE.

- NOTICE AT WHAT POINT YOU WOULD NORMALLY GIVE UP AND PUSH YOURSELF THAT BIT FURTHER. STICKABILITY IS A QUALITY THAT INCREASES OUR LEVELS OF HAPPINESS AND HOPEFULNESS. AS WE RECOGNISE OUR INNER STRENGTHS WE BEGIN TO DEVELOP DEEPER LEVELS OF SELF-APPRECIATION AND TRUST. WE KNOW THAT WE WILL NEVER LET OURSELVES DOWN AND THIS IS SUCH A GREAT FEELING!

Hopeful people

Christopher Reeve said that hope is a choice and so it seems to be. But why would we ever choose to feel hopeless rather than hopeful? What would be the point in feeling miserable when we could be feeling happy? Why do some people seem to be able to choose to feel happy, hopeful and optimistic whilst others appear to be choosing to feel unhappy, hopeless and pessimistic?

We are creatures of habit and we have learned many coping strategies and some of these are not necessarily helpful. If we are used to adopting a self-doubting and negative approach then this will become second nature to us; we will take a cynical and downbeat line just because that is what we have always done. Start noticing the different ways that friends and relatives tackle their own challenges. Who do you know who always seems to find a positive way through? And who is it that always looks on the bleak side of life?

Experts agree that it takes twenty-one days to change an old habit and to reinforce a new one. This is liberating news because it means that in a short time you can change the way that you think and by doing this you can change the way you feel and the way that you behave. If you are locked in negative beliefs about yourself and the rest of the world you will find that hopefulness is an elusive state. But all is not lost! Begin to break that pessimistic habit right now. Choose optimism instead, even if this feels very hard to do. Practise being hopeful in the face of adversity; be positive rather than negative and expect the best to happen. If you stick at this then you will feel the changes quite soon. Choose hope and go for your dreams and you will feel focused, energetic and enthusiastic about life. If Christopher Reeve could do this then you can too.

10 ways to rekindle hope

1 **Seek it.** Even if you cannot see a silver lining at the moment, start to look for it. Our intention helps to create our outcomes and a strong desire to lift your energy will lighten your mood.

2 **Appreciate the beauty of nature.** Spend time out of doors and you will return feeling more grounded and peaceful and connected with life. Appreciation always creates an optimistic mood and fresh air and birdsong are great enliveners.

3 **Write a letter to a friend.** We are inclined to get back from life whatever we give. Each time we reach out to another person we experience the very basic human joy of sharing ourselves. Give that bit more than a text or email requires and you will feel the benefits.

4 **Step out of hopelessness.** Whenever negative clouds begin to close in, take a realistic look at your self-doubts. Rise above your lack of sparkle by finding something to value in your life.

5 **Do something physical.** Despondency can trap our minds in a seemingly never-ending cycle. If we dignify this mood with too much mental attention any hopeful tendencies will disappear. When it all gets too much stop analysing and get your body working. Physical exercise is sometimes all we need to shift bleak energy into something more purposeful and engaging.

6 **Use bright and positive language.** Enthusiastic speech creates an energy all of its own. Lift your tone and your vocabulary and you will immediately feel better.

7 **Remind yourself that everything changes.** However troublesome things might be, they will not stay the same. Optimists stay mindful of this fact even when times are very difficult. Try this approach, it really does work.

8 **Enjoy something.** This might seem like odd advice to give to someone in despair, but actually it works because of its sheer simplicity. If you can engage in a moment of joy you will become more hopeful immediately. So watch a favourite movie; eat a Häagen Dazs sorbet; wear your favourite strappy sandals . . . . tune into anything that you love and watch those blues disappear.

9 **Encourage someone else.** This is a foolproof way to make you feel better. As soon as you tap into the encouraging habit you will miraculously find yourself feeling encouraged too. This tip will never fail to warm the cockles of your heart and open you to a hopeful state once more.

10 **Look at the bigger picture.** A low mood tends to make our world shrink as we focus more and more minutely on our perceived problems. If you are tied up in knots over an issue at the moment take a step back and view the situation from a wider perspective. If it remains a serious concern then take action to deal with it as soon as possible, and if it's not then just let it go.

R E F R E S H   A N D   R E N E W

YOUR TREE OF LIFE

IN MANY TRADITIONS THE TREE IS USED AS A METAPHOR FOR LIFE. RELAX AND CLOSE YOUR EYES AND IMAGINE WHAT YOUR TREE OF LIFE MIGHT LOOK LIKE.

- BECOME AWARE OF THE ROOTS OF WHO YOU ARE. REFLECT UPON HOW YOU HAVE YOU BEEN INFLUENCED BY YOUR FAMILY AND YOUR EARLY ENVIRONMENT. NOTICE HOW YOUR ROOTS ANCHOR YOU TO THE GROUND AND GIVE YOU STABILITY.

- NOW LOOK AT YOUR TRUNK; SEE THE MARKS ON THE BARK AND NOTICE THE SCARS THAT YOU HAVE GATHERED AS YOU HAVE DEVELOPED AND GROWN. ARE THERE ANY WOUNDS THAT STILL HAVEN'T HEALED?

- SEE THE LEAVES AND THE BUDS THAT ARE FORMING. THESE BUDS ARE YOUR HOPES AND DREAMS THAT WILL ONE DAY COME TO FRUITION; NURTURE THEM AND THEY WILL BLOSSOM INTO YOUR FUTURE.

- AND NOW LOOK AT THE FRUITS OF YOUR TREE; THESE ARE YOUR SUCCESSES AND ACHIEVEMENTS. LOOK HOW COLOURFUL AND SPLENDID THEY ARE. SPEND SOME TIME APPRECIATING THE FRUITS OF YOUR LABOUR.

- FINALLY, IMAGINE YOUR TREE IN WINTER WITH ITS BARE BRANCHES, STANDING SILENT AND PROUD. AND KNOW THAT EVEN IN THE DARKEST DAYS YOUR TREE IS BUZZING WITH INNER LIFE AS IT PREPARES ITSELF FOR A NEW AND HOPEFUL SPRING.

- ADMIRE THE STRENGTH, VIGOUR AND PURPOSE OF YOUR TREE.

Day 6 TODAY'S HAPPINESS ROUNDUP

Again it's time to reflect on your day. Circle your score and fill out the sections in your journal.

MY HAPPINESS SCORE FOR THE DAY

TOTALLY   FABULOUS
  FED-UP
    1   2   3   4   5   6   7   8   9   10

Most significant event of the day
....
....

My main concern of the day
....
....

What can I do about this, if anything?
....
....

Most useful happiness strategies today
....
....

What went well today
....
....

Three things that made me smile today

....

....

Has anything else been significant today? If so, make a note of it.

Final reflections

- Cheerfulness and contentment are great beautifiers.
- None of us is perfect so give yourself a well-deserved break.
- You can do whatever it takes to take charge of your life.
- As soon as we are ready to look for it that spark of hopefulness is always there shining brightly.
- The more you can trust yourself the happier you will feel.

Love is All You Need

It is the loving, not the loved, woman who feels lovable.

JESSAMYN WEST

Many people die with their music still in them.
Why is this so? Too often it is because they are
always getting ready to live. Before they know it,
time runs out.

Oliver Wendell Holmes

Is your life on hold? Are you waiting for something to happen
or for someone to do something before you can really get
going? If you are, then consider the implications of this. The
only time you can be certain of is this very instant, and the
most important question to ask yourself is: am I living this
moment to the max? But we often get so lost in our day-to-
day affairs that weeks or even months can pass by in a haze
of automatic responses and habitual behaviours. If you are
feeling bored or disenchanted then use these feelings as a
wake-up call; something in your life needs changing and now
is the time to cut to the chase.

Buckminster Fuller was an architect, engineer and visionary
and one of the most original thinkers of the second half of the
twentieth century. He conceived of man as a passenger in a
cosmic spaceship, whose only wealth consists in energy and
information. I like this definition of our assets and it fits well
with the self-help theme of this book. In fact Fuller goes on to
say that '. . . there is one outstandingly important fact regarding

Spaceship Earth, and that is that no instruction manual came with it'. But of course we can learn to understand our energy and gather information about the way that we operate and in this way we can create a manual for ourselves.

We can think of happiness as a DIY project where, given the right materials, we can create a joyful and satisfying life for ourselves and those around us. What raw materials are you working with? Are you thinking your way to happiness or to sadness? Are you relishing your moments or are you irritably rushing from one task to another? Is your heart full of joy or full of despair? Do you love your life? Why wait for a health scare before you appreciate what you have? If you were told that your life was nearly at an end how would your perceptions change? Would you do things differently? Well, let's face this truth today: your life will end and you don't know when, so decide to start living and loving it now. You have nothing to lose and everything to gain. Don't let time run out before you have sung all your songs and played all your tunes.

We have so much to give to life and often our unhappiness develops because we are not firing on all cylinders; we are running below capacity and we know it. The more we put into things the more we get back and so today we are going to concentrate on putting more love into our life.

CHANGE ONE THING

GIVE YOURSELF SOME LOVE

WE ARE LOVE-SEEKING MISSILES, SEARCHING FOR ADMIRATION AND APPRECIATION FROM THOSE AROUND US. IF YOU DON'T BELIEVE THIS JUST START NOTICING HOW WONDERFUL YOU FEEL WHEN YOU ARE ADMIRED AND

SUPPORTED BY OTHERS. AND ALSO THINK ABOUT HOW YOU FEEL WHEN OTHERS SHOW THEIR DISAPPROVAL.

BUT SOMETIMES WE SACRIFICE OURSELVES FOR THE APPROVAL OF OTHERS, DOING OR SAYING THINGS TO PLEASE OTHER PEOPLE RATHER THAN TO PLEASE OURSELVES. WE ARE INCLINED TO DO THIS WHEN WE ARE FEELING INSECURE AND UNHAPPY WITH OURSELVES. WHEN WE FEEL HIGH IN SELF-ESTEEM WE DON'T NEED OTHERS TO SHOW US HOW GREAT WE ARE BECAUSE WE KNOW OUR OWN SELF-WORTH.

- START TO LOVE AND VALUE YOURSELF. TRY LOOKING IN A MIRROR AND GAZING INTO YOUR EYES. LOOK LONG AND HARD AND SEE THE AMAZING PERSON WHO IS LOOKING BACK AT YOU.

- GIVE YOURSELF A HUG; WRAP YOUR ARMS AROUND YOURSELF AND SQUEEZE TIGHT; YOU ARE DOING SO WELL YOU CAN BE PROUD OF YOURSELF.

- STOP TREATING YOURSELF BADLY; YOU REALLY DO DESERVE THE BEST. GIVE YOURSELF A BREAK TODAY AND HAVE A DAY OFF FROM SELF-CRITICISM. YOU WILL FEEL SO MUCH FREER AND BRIGHTER.

- ADMIRE YOUR STRENGTH OF PURPOSE AND YOUR DETERMINATION AS YOU WORK THROUGH THIS BOOK. HAPPINESS IS A CHOICE AND YOU HAVE CHOSEN TO GO FOR IT.

Feel good and do good and feel even better!

Psychologists recognise that when we feel good we are more inclined to reach out to others and this in turn increases our good feelings; they call this the feel-good, do-good phenomenon. It does us good to be kind and it even does us good to witness people being kind to others; kindness has a domino effect and one small caring deed can lead on to countless other acts of thoughtfulness. Psychologist Jonathan Haidt talks about the way that we can feel 'elevated' by observing the helpfulness of others and how this feeling makes us more open, considerate and loving to the rest of humanity. Perhaps you can experience that feeling of elevation (or spiritual upliftment) as you read this remarkable story.

Shmuel Greenbaum is fighting terror with kindness in the ultimate act of forgiveness. On 9 August 2001 Shmuel's wife Shoshana was murdered by a suicide bomber at the Sbarro restaurant in Jerusalem; over 100 people were killed or injured on that day. Shmuel says, 'Sometimes I wonder whether telling my story can really help others. Since the way I am coping with tragedy is so different than the norm, would anyone else understand it? After my wife's violent murder, I began a project to teach people to be kinder. The project has just started to take off. At the moment, we have more than 40,000 subscribers on six continents to our "Daily Dose of Kindness" email.'

This man has turned his personal tragedy into a wonderful story of hope and love. He searched for a way to climb out of his despair and really did create his own very original and inspired DIY manual for happiness. There really is so much good in the world when we start to look for it, isn't there? Love makes the world go round and love *is* everywhere!

Take a look again at the Cycle of Happiness diagram on page 22 This cycle of positivity is rooted in love – love of self, the universe and all that dwells in it. Whenever we find ourselves stuck in the negative Cycle of Unhappiness we can lift ourselves into the positive cycle by touching the love we find in our hearts and souls. When we are choosing to come from a loving space we embrace an expansive awareness; our minds and our hearts are open and we are able to feel compassion for ourselves and others. The Beatles were right: love is all you need.

If you are searching for happiness at the moment just stop and consider your thoughts and your feelings. How much love is in your life right now? Why not increase the love in your heart by thinking of someone who you care for? Touch those loving feelings and let them expand. Look around you and give thanks for what you have; feel the appreciation growing in your heart. Remember that you are doing your best and let yourself off the hook; love your human weaknesses. Is there anyone in your life who you are angry with? If so just imagine those angry thoughts floating away and leaving you with a feeling of kindness. Love is a feeling that is inside you and you can touch it whenever you wish. And whenever you give your loving thoughts attention then they grow even more; keep watering your seeds of love.

HAPPINESS TIP

NOTICE THE LOVE AROUND YOU

When we are downbeat we are inclined to feel that there is something missing in our lives and if we dwell on this then things only get worse. We know that a preoccupation with unhappiness and negativity will create more of the same and that if we concentrate on the positive then we will feel more optimistic. If your life feels lacking in something then try filling that space with love. Begin to notice the love that surrounds you. Look for loving gestures as you go about your day:

- The young man who gives up his seat for an older woman.

- A group of friends laughing together.

- The friendly smile of the newsagent when you buy the paper.

- The small child throwing a stick for his dog in the park.

- Your neighbour's cheery 'good morning'.

- The kindness of a work colleague who brings you a cup of tea.

- The phone call from a friend who wants to know how you are.

RECOGNISE AND APPRECIATE ANY ACT OF LOVE THAT YOU SEE. THE MORE YOU LOOK FOR LOVE THE MORE IT WILL MANIFEST, AND AS IT DOES THE BETTER YOU WILL FEEL. BELIEVE THAT LOVE IS EVERYWHERE AND YOU WILL SEE IT IN THE MOST UNEXPECTED PLACES. MAKE SOME NOTES IN YOUR JOURNAL ABOUT WHAT YOU SEE AND HOW LOVING YOU FEEL TODAY.

The gift of forgiveness

After all the years that I have worked in personal development, searching for practices and strategies that work to increase wellbeing and happiness, I still value one practice above all others. For me, forgiveness is the most vibrant and life-changing procedure; it never fails to lift the spirits and lighten our lives and touch our hearts with love; it moves negative energy faster than any technique I know and it brings with it the wonderful gifts of peace, calm, balance and compassion.

People often react strongly to the concept of forgiveness, feeling that they have a right to hold on to their anger towards another who has treated them badly. And of course we are angry when we feel victimised. But if we continually hold on to that initial anger we can never be at our brightest and happiest. The quality of our thoughts creates the quality of our lives and if we hang on to past hurts and slights our anger only grows and hurts us even more. So think of forgiveness as a means of letting go of negative energy and opening yourself up to a happier future. As Archbishop Desmond Tutu says, 'To forgive is not just to be altruistic, it is the best form of self-interest.'

I often hear clients talk over and over again about people who have hurt and upset them; they sometimes spend more time thinking about these people than they do about those who care for them and support them. If we cannot forgive (let go) of those who have upset us then we carry forever the memory of them and the pain that they inflicted upon us. This is a heavy negative load to bear but it is possible to release this burden however badly we have been treated. Forgiveness of others calls for a radical rethink of your past hurts; it doesn't mean that you don't care about how others behaved towards you. In fact it means exactly the opposite: you care enough to reconsider whatever happened in order to be able to finally let it rest.

Are you holding angry thoughts about someone? If so, would you like to find a creative way to let them go?

The four steps to forgiveness

(Adapted from my book, *Just Do It Now!*)

Step 1 **State the facts.** View whatever happened as objectively as possible. At first you might have to pretend that it happened to someone else in order to get a true perspective. Write down the facts in your journal. Stick to the reality and don't embroider it with your emotions. So, for example, you might write, *my mother was an alcoholic when I was growing up.*

Step 2 **Accept the facts.** Don't get lost in blame and tears; you are no longer a victim of the past. A creative response (non-blaming) will allow you to move forward and leave the hurt behind, so be creative in your approach.

If you need to express your feelings about what happened then make sure you do this, but don't get stuck in repeated emotional discharge (this might feel like you are working through something when you are really only going over the same old issue).

Step 3 **Decide to let go.** This is a defining moment. Are you ready to let go or are you still gaining more from moaning, blaming and feeling angry? Once you have definitely confirmed your desire to forgive, then the process really starts moving. Don't expect 100 per cent success immediately, it might take a while. Sometimes it's only possible to forgive a bit at a time (I can forgive *this* but not *that* at the moment). Later you might bring yourself to let go of *that*, but only if you hang on to something else. Forgiveness is a process that has a profound curative effect on the wounds of the past and eventually these wounds can be healed.

Step 4 **Enjoy the freedom** that forgiveness brings. The more you can forgive the better you will feel about yourself and the rest of the world, and as you let go of pain your heart will fill with love and peace. Forgiveness is the ultimate gift as it brings love to both the forgiver and the forgiven.

The F word

You might feel even more inspired to get going on your forgiveness work if you visit www.theforgivenessproject.com. This site tells the story of the The Forgiveness Project, a charitable organisation that works with grassroots projects in the areas of conflict resolution, reconciliation and victim support. Its patrons include Archbishop Desmond Tutu, Anita Roddick and Emma Thompson and its work reaches out to people right across the globe. The F Word is the name given to the project's touring exhibition of personal accounts of reconciliation and renewal and includes the amazing stories of both perpetrators and victims. Visit the site and click on 'stories' and you will find an array of incredible personal journeys towards the forgiveness of others and also towards self-forgiveness.

The depths of our patience, tolerance and forgiveness of others is a reflection of the patience, tolerance and forgiveness that we feel for ourselves. In the words of writer Eric Hoffer: 'The remarkable thing is that we really love our neighbour as ourselves: we do unto others as we do unto ourselves. We hate others when we hate ourselves. We are tolerant toward others when we tolerate ourselves. We forgive others when we forgive ourselves. We are prone to sacrifice others when we are ready to sacrifice ourselves.'

ACTIVITY: SENDING LOVINGKINDNESS

THE LOVINGKINDNESS MEDITATION IS A GENTLE AND POWERFUL BUDDHIST MEDITATION THAT CAN BE USED AT ANY TIME AND IN ANY PLACE. THIS SIMPLE VARIATION IS ONE THAT WILL INCREASE YOUR OWN FEELINGS OF LOVE AND HAPPINESS AND WILL ALSO REACH OUT AND POSITIVELY AFFECT OTHERS.

- RELAX COMFORTABLY, CLOSE YOUR EYES AND TURN YOUR ATTENTION INWARD.

- BEGIN WITH SENDING LOVINGKINDNESS TO YOURSELF. SAY TO YOURSELF, 'MAY I FEEL HAPPY, KIND, JOYFUL AND LOVING.' REPEAT THIS TEN TIMES.

- NOW IMAGINE SOMEONE WHO YOU CARE ABOUT; SEE THEM IN YOUR MIND'S EYE AND SAY, 'MAY YOU FEEL HAPPY, KIND, JOYFUL AND LOVING.' REPEAT THIS TEN TIMES.

- NEXT CONSIDER SOMEONE WHO YOU ARE FINDING IT DIFFICULT TO GET ALONG WITH. VISUALISE THIS PERSON AND SAY, 'MAY YOU FEEL HAPPY, KIND, JOYFUL AND LOVING.' REPEAT AS BEFORE.

IF AT ANY TIME YOU FIND THAT YOU ARE DRIFTING OFF AND LOSING CONCENTRATION JUST BRING YOURSELF GENTLY BACK AND CONTINUE. DON'T BE SURPRISED IF YOU DISCOVER A RELUCTANCE TO SAY THESE WORDS, EITHER TO YOURSELF OR TO OTHERS. SOMETIMES WHEN WE SEND LOVINGKINDNESS WE CREATE A BIT OF A BACKLASH AS NEGATIVE FEELINGS ARISE. IF THIS HAPPENS (FOR EXAMPLE, *I DON'T DESERVE TO BE HAPPY OR SHE DOESN'T DESERVE TO BE JOYFUL*) JUST NOTICE THESE FEELINGS AND RETURN TO THE MEDITATION. IT IS INTERESTING THAT MANY PEOPLE FIND THAT IT IS SO MUCH EASIER TO WISH FOR GOOD THINGS FOR OTHERS RATHER THAN FOR THEMSELVES, BUT OF COURSE WE CAN ONLY GIVE TO OTHERS WHAT WE ALREADY HAVE OURSELVES. WHEN YOUR OWN HEART IS FILLED WITH LOVINGKINDNESS YOU WILL BE FULL OF GOODWILL TO OTHERS.

TRY THIS MEDITATION IN A WORK MEETING (NO NEED TO CLOSE YOUR EYES OF COURSE). JUST INWARDLY FOCUS

When blame gets in the way

When we are feeling fed-up we often look around for a
scapegoat to hold responsible. We might blame a person or
Fate or the weather or bad luck or whatever is most
convenient. Initially the blaming makes us feel better as we
throw our focus and attention away from our own miserable
mood and on to something or someone else. But this relief is
only ever temporary. The blaming game is not a creative
response because it actually blocks our potential to change
and improve our situation. If the fault lies with anyone or
anything else then we remain dependent on those outside
forces to change; in other words, we have given away our
control, and this makes us even more unhappy. Notice the
next time that you are inclined to give away your power in
this way. Start to become aware of this habit and to recognise
how blaming always stops you making a genuine and loving
response.

Rosa's story

I met Rosa a few years ago when she came on a relationships
workshop that I was running in London. She was in her early
thirties, happily married with two children and worked as a
dance and movement therapist. Everything about her life was

going well and yet she said that she felt unhappy at a very deep level. As the workshop moved into the afternoon we started to talk about the need for forgiveness in families particularly in relation to parents and siblings. I find that quite a lot of people have some unfinished business with members of their very close family and this often reveals itself on a day-long programme.

Rosa revealed that she had not spoken to her older sister Helen for about six years and that she felt a lot of hatred and anger towards her. Rosa felt that she had grown up in Helen's shadow and was never able to be as good as her older sister at school, in sport or in anything. In tears Rosa said: 'She (Helen) was the golden girl, my parents' favourite, who could never do anything wrong. I spent my childhood just running to keep up with my sister, I was always competing with her and it was so frustrating because I could never win. She even got a place at Cambridge University while I flunked the entrance exam. We had a great blow up at my wedding when I told her to get out of my life and she left the reception and we haven't spoken since. A couple of years ago she had a miscarriage but I just couldn't swallow my hurt and pride and so I didn't make contact with her and she has never met my girls. I have been sitting here thinking about how my heart feels so hard and rigid most of the time. I find it impossible to get in touch with my emotions and I wonder if it's because I am carrying all this baggage about Helen. Once or twice my husband has suggested that I call her up or invite her and her husband over but I just couldn't bear the thought of it. But today I feel different, especially as I have heard other people talk about how letting go of the past has helped them to move on. And I wonder what my daughters will think of me when they find out that they have an aunt who they've never met. I would hate my girls to fall out the way we have. I can't carry on acting like a child, it's time I grew up and moved on from this. I've decided to get in touch with Helen and somehow I feel so much better already. Perhaps if I can stop blaming her for the past I might be able to forgive myself. I've become bitter and how can I love and accept myself when I'm so full of hatred?'

When we are full of pain it can feel impossible to open up to anyone, let alone those who we think have helped cause our sadness. But it's only when we begin to let love in that we can start to heal. The ability to forgive others allows us to feel better about ourselves and it is in this way that forgiveness works its most wonderful magic. We all need the transforming power of love in our lives and when you can open up your heart you will indeed feel fabulous.

Writing in her *Present Moments* newsletter in April 2006 Louise Hay offers this simple yet profound insight. 'There's so much love in this world, and there's so much love in my heart, but sometimes I forget. Sometimes I think there isn't enough, or that there's just a small amount, so I hoard what I have or I'm afraid to let it go. If there's a belief within me that says: *I can't have*, or *I'm not good enough*, I think to myself: I am willing to let that belief go. I don't have to believe that anymore. I don't have to struggle. It's not hard work. I'm just changing a thought.'

Decide to change any negative thoughts that might be limiting your wonderful potential. There is indeed so much love in this world; don't ever forget this. When you can believe in love then love will come to you.

Try making any of the following affirmations:

Love is everywhere
I love my life
My heart is open to love
I deserve love.
I forgive myself
I believe in love
Love makes the world go round
Love is all we need
I am full of love

CHANGE ONE THING

BY TAKING THE JOYFUL PATH

JOY AND STRUGGLE ARE NOT THE RESULTS OF THINGS HAPPENING TO YOU, THEY ARE ONLY ATTITUDES AND APPROACHES AND YOU ARE ALWAYS FREE TO CHOOSE ONE OR THE OTHER. WHY CHOOSE TO BE MISERABLE WHEN YOU CAN BE HAPPY? WHY NOT TAKE OFF THOSE GLOOMY DARK GLASSES AND TRY ON SOME ROSE-TINTED SPECS? GIVE UP THE STRUGGLE JUST FOR TODAY AND TRY THE PATH OF JOY.

- IMAGINE THAT YOU ARE STANDING AT AN INTERSECTION AND ONE ROUTE IS THE PATH OF STRUGGLE AND THE OTHER IS THE PATH OF JOY.

- SUSPEND ALL CYNICISM, FEAR AND DISBELIEF AND LET HAPPINESS INTO YOUR HEART BY CHOOSING TO TAKE THE JOYFUL PATH.

- TAKE YOUR JOYFUL CONSCIOUSNESS OUT INTO THE WORLD.

- IF YOU HEAR SOMEONE MOANING AND COMPLAINING JUST RECOGNISE THE PATH OF STRUGGLE AND DON'T GO DOWN THERE. STAY IN THE MOMENT AND KEEP LOOKING FOR THE JOYFUL ROUTE THROUGH.

- IF SOMEONE TREATS YOU BADLY DON'T JOIN THEM ON THAT NEGATIVE PATH; JUST FOR TODAY TRY TURNING THE OTHER CHEEK.

- DON'T LET YOURSELF BE DISTRACTED BY THE ACTIONS AND EMOTIONS OF OTHERS; STAY IN YOUR CALM AND HAPPY CENTRE.

- TRY THIS FOR ONE DAY AND SEE HOW IT WORKS. DON'T LET YOURSELF BE TRAPPED BY YOUR THOUGHTS AND FEAR, CHOOSE TO FEEL UPLIFTED INSTEAD.

- EVERY TIME YOU RADIATE JOY YOU ATTRACT IT BACK TO YOU IN EVEN GREATER MEASURE. WHO KNOWS, ONE JOYFUL DAY MIGHT JUST LEAD TO ANOTHER.

Make a difference by spreading your love around

We have seen how long-lasting happiness is linked with a feeling of being creatively engaged in our life and when we are doing what we love to do we are happy. Research shows that when we feel we are making a difference in some way this gives us as added meaning and purpose. We could describe the act of 'making a difference' as being an expression of our love for life and for others.

Camilla Batmanghelidjh is the founder of Kids Company (www.kidsco.org.uk), which is a charity that helps vulnerable children, providing them with care and practical help. In an interview with *Psychologies* magazine Camilla, who was voted Social Entrepreneur of the Year in 2005, said: 'I will die in a rocking chair with no material goods, and if I died tomorrow I would be happy . . . I decided not to have a family because I have a very vocational psyche. I just want to get this done. I know what I've chosen feels right; very few people get to live their dream.' When she was nine years old Camilla knew how she would spend her life. Even though her family didn't take her seriously she wrote the working model for Kids Company when she was fourteen.

Perhaps you are thinking that you would love to live your own dream if only you knew what it was. A good way to begin your search is to look closely at where your passions lie. Take another look at '10 ways to get back on track', on page 114. What do you love to do? How can you do more of it? Could you share this wonderful creative energy of yours; can you spread your love around? There are so many ways to share ourselves with others; here is an unusual and creative example of how it's possible to help to improve the lives of others by indulging in what you love to do.

London's Guerrilla Gardeners are busy transforming neglected public spaces into places of beauty. The movement began in 2004 when Richard Reynolds, an Oxford graduate-turned-advertising trainee, decided to cheer up the desolate garden outside the South London tower block where he has a flat. After he had weeded and planted it he discovered that other people were interested in brightening up the environment and the volunteers have gone from strength to strength. As the guerrilla gardeners' projects bloom, more and more people are joining in to help. Richard says that he inherited his passion for gardening from his mother and that the guerrillas are, '. . . ordinary people but just look at what ordinary people can do when they get together . . .' What a great way to spread some seeds of happiness.

REFRESH AND RENEW

CULTIVATING A LOVING HEART

When you can connect with the love in your heart you tap into a deep, intuitive inner wisdom. Try these simple ways to increase your loving connection.

- Think of three times in the past when you experienced a rush of loving feelings when you talked to someone or thought about them. Really get into the skin of what this felt like.

- Think of three people you know who are in need of love right now. Bring to mind the loving feelings that you have just remembered. Send this love out to these three people. Don't be concerned about how to do this, just imagine the love flowing from your heart to them. Your intention will move the energy.

- Recollect three times when someone gave you love that you were not expecting. What did they do to delight and surprise you?

- CONSIDER A WAY THAT YOU COULD SURPRISE SOMEONE YOU KNOW WITH AN UNEXPECTED DEMONSTRATION OF YOUR LOVE. NOW DO THIS AS SOON AS POSSIBLE.

- THE MORE LOVE YOU GIVE TO LIFE THE MORE LOVE LIFE GIVES YOU BACK. KEEP WITH THE LOVING FEELINGS!

Day 7 TODAY'S HAPPINESS ROUNDUP

Again it's time to reflect on your day. Circle your score and fill out the sections in your journal.

MY HAPPINESS SCORE FOR THE DAY

TOTALLY   FABULOUS
FED-UP

1   2   3   4   5   6   7   8   9   10

Most significant event of the day

....

....

My main concern of the day

....

....

What can I do about this, if anything?

....

....

Most useful happiness strategies today

....

....

What went well today

....

....

Three things that made me smile today

....

....

As before, take a few moments to think about and make a
note of anything that made a particular impact on you today.

Final reflections

- The more we put into life the more we get back.
- Happiness is a choice and you have chosen to go for it.
- When you give your loving thoughts attention they
  grow, so keep watering the seeds of love.
- The depths of our patience, tolerance and forgiveness
  of others is a reflection of the patience, tolerance and
  forgiveness that we feel for ourselves.
- Whenever we strive to 'make a difference' we are
  expressing our love of life and our love for others.

Don't Forget to Have Fun!

Good humour is very inexpensive. It is one of the pleasures in life that is relatively free. I'm sure, if we try hard enough, we can remember a part of us that used to laugh and be playful.

ANNE WILSON SCHAEF

I've learned that you can tell a lot about a person by the way he or she handles these three things: a rainy day, lost luggage, and tangled Christmas tree lights.

MAYA ANGELOU

When Oprah interviewed Maya Angelou on her seventy-second birthday the great poet and author made this wonderful seriously playful comment. We do indeed show our true colours when faced with the minor inconveniences in life and it's how we deal with the detail that creates the true quality of our overall experience.

When I first met my husband he called around one morning when my washing machine had flooded the flat. There I was, mop in hand and ankle deep in water trying to get my two small children to stop splashing around in it. I was way past trying to make a great impression and I remember thinking, well if he can't take this at least I'm going to find out now. He might have taken one look and been frightened off forever by the three of us but instead he laughed his head off and made a game of clearing it all up. At that moment I knew he was the right man for me. His great sense of humour and love of life have played a big part in making our long marriage such a success.

Of course our mood can often dictate the way we deal with everyday hassles, so that a wet day can either find us singing in the rain (feeling happy) or moaning under our umbrella (obviously not feeling happy). But to put it all in perspective we might do well to heed the wise words of Billy Connolly who reminds us that: 'There is no such thing as bad weather – only the wrong clothes.' So, rather than letting a bad mood lead us into even more irritation and frustration we could just choose to change our attitude to the way we handle difficult unforeseen circumstances.

How fun-filled is your life at the moment? Try the Christmas tree lights test and be honest with your answer. Well, would the tangled strands drive you into a frenzy or would you just take a deep breath and start unravelling them? You will discover a link between the amount of fun in your life and the degree of calm and equanimity that you have at your disposal:

MORE FUN → FEELING OF HAPPINESS → ABILITY TO KEEP THINGS IN PERSPECTIVE → FEELING OF CALM AND BEING IN CONTROL

LESS FUN → FEELING OF UNHAPPINESS → UNABLE TO SEE THE BIGGER PICTURE → FEELING OF FRUSTRATION AND LOSS OF CONTROL

It's not possible to be unhappy and miserable when you are having fun. Enjoyment, laughter and pleasure causes a release of endorphins, those wonderful brain chemicals that fill us with feelings of wellbeing and bonhomie. But when we are low and anxious we are less likely to be looking for fun-filled activities and more likely to be withdrawing into our negative thoughts.

CHANGE ONE THING

STOP SWEATING THE SMALL STUFF

WHEN THE PRESSURE MOUNTS AND OUR STRESS LEVELS RISE WE ARE INCLINED TO TAKE EVERYTHING A BIT TOO SERIOUSLY. WHEN THIS HAPPENS OUR IRRITATION LEVELS SHOOT SKY HIGH AND BEFORE WE KNOW IT WE ARE FEELING ANNOYED AND UPSET AT THE SLIGHTEST INCONVENIENCE.

- WHEN YOU NEXT FIND YOURSELF GETTING WOUND UP OVER SOMETHING JUST STOP AND ASK YOURSELF THIS QUESTION: 'DOES IT REALLY MATTER?'

- IF YOU THINK IT DOES THEN FOLLOW THIS UP WITH ANOTHER QUESTION: 'WILL THIS MATTER NEXT WEEK?'

- AND IF IT DOES STILL MATTER THEN GET TO GRIPS WITH WHAT MUST BE DONE (APPROPRIATE ACTION IS A PERFECT REMEDY FOR STRESS).

BEFORE YOU NEXT BREAK OUT INTO A SWEAT OVER SOMETHING, CHECK ON ITS 'MATTERABILITY'. FAR FROM IT MATTERING NEXT WEEK, THE CHANCES ARE THAT YOU WON'T EVEN REMEMBER IT.

LOOK AFTER YOUR MENTAL HEALTH BY TAKING THE TIME TO GET THINGS INTO PERSPECTIVE. YOU WILL PAY A HIGH PRICE IF YOU KEEP LETTING YOURSELF FLY OFF THE HANDLE AT EVERY TURN: OVERREACTION INCREASES IRRITATION LEVELS, WHICH VERY QUICKLY LEAD INTO NEGATIVITY AND FEELINGS OF LOW SELF-WORTH AND UNHAPPINESS.

Use it or lose it

It's easy to think that fun things happen to happy people and miserable things happen to unhappy people. But let's look at this another way. We know that the mental states of happiness and unhappiness are choices that we make; we can think ourselves happy or sad because happiness is a state of mind and not an external force. And we also know that having more fun increases our capacity for happiness. So, rather than sit in our misery waiting for fun to arrive (highly unlikely!) we could choose to increase the pleasure content of our days and thereby increase our happiness levels. If we don't keep using our capacity to see the lighter side of life and to enjoy ourselves then we will begin to lose this important ability. As with many things in life, if we don't use it (our sense of humour) we will lose it!

Have you noticed how some people appear to naturally attract enjoyment and pleasure while others seem almost determined not to have a good time? But glance through the personal ads in any paper or magazine and it will be hard to find a person who isn't looking for someone with a GSOH. The truth is that we are attracted to people who enjoy life; we love the way their qualities of enthusiasm and humour rub off on us and lift our spirits. And the wet blankets just don't have the same effect on us, do they?

Quick quiz: are you having enough fun?

Look at the following questions, choosing answers A or B or C.

1 How would you describe yourself?

A   I'm a pleasure seeker.

B   I'm a serious person.

C   I'm bit of both.

2 How much leisure time do you have each week?

A   More than 10 hours.

B   I don't have any free time for pure enjoyment.

C   I grab the odd half hour here and there each day.

3 When did you last have a really good laugh?

A   Yesterday.

B   I can't remember.

C   A week or two ago.

4 Which of theses 3 words do you most associate with the concept of fun?

A   Joyfulness.

B   Frivolity.

C   Happiness.

5 When did you last watch one of your favourite comedy shows?

A   In the last week.

B   I don't watch comedy shows.

C   A week or two ago.

6 Have you heard the one about . . .?

A   Yes I have and I know a good one too.

B   No and my heart sinks at the prospect of having to listen to it.

C   I might have but I don't mind listening to it again.

7 Can you name a favourite friend who can always make you smile?

A Yes, I have a few.

B No.

C Yes.

8 When did you last do something just for a laugh?

A Recently.

B I don't do anything just for the fun of it.

C Some time ago.

9 You catch a stranger's eye for a moment, do you smile?

A Usually.

B No, I don't smile at strangers.

C Occasionally.

10 You have been invited to a fancy dress party, how do you feel?

A Delighted, I can't wait to dress up.

B Unhappy, I will feel ridiculous in fancy dress.

C A bit unsure but the idea will probably grow on me.

If you scored mainly As

You are most likely to be: a spontaneous and carefree person. Yes, you are having plenty of fun and are probably very positive. You love enjoying yourself and will do almost anything for a laugh.

Be aware that: your extrovert tendencies might overwhelm some people, so remember to remain sensitive to the feelings of others if you think that this is happening; let the quieter ones take the centre of attention occasionally.

Do this: Carry on being your usual friendly self, spread the fun around and help to lighten the mood of others; you are good at this.

If you scored mainly Bs

You are most likely to be: rather serious and maybe a bit withdrawn. You are quite shy and possibly struggle to make friends. You take life ultra seriously and don't like the idea of indulging in any time-wasting activities.

Be aware that: this approach is not good for your emotional health. When we lose our sense of humour we are inclined to become very negative and inward looking.

Do this: Find your sense of humour, it hasn't left you completely. Go out and do something just for the fun of it and see how this feels. If you want to be happy then you must start to bring more pleasure into your life; you deserve this.

If you scored mainly Cs

You are most likely to be: a busy person with a lot of responsibilities. You know how to have fun but time is probably an issue for you. You like leisure activities and wish you could take more time out.

Be aware that: you can only give to others if you remember to nurture yourself. If you are running a fun deficit then you will be resentful and angry and this will eventually lead to all sorts of unhappiness.

Do this: Get your time management issues under control and schedule FUN activities into your diary. Start delegating and asking for help if necessary. Next time you are feeling unhappy recognise that this is because you are *not having enough fun;* then do something about this right away.

HAPPINESS TIP

TRANSCEND YOUR WORRIES

WORRIES, NIGGLES AND UPSETS CAN CERTAINLY TAKE THE FUN OUT OF LIVING. BUT THEN LIFE IS ALWAYS COMING UP WITH SOME CHALLENGE OR OTHER TO ENGAGE US SO WE NEED A WAY TO TRANSCEND THE EVERYDAY STRESSES AND STRAINS. HERE IS A GREAT TIP THAT WILL ALWAYS HELP YOU TO RISE ABOVE YOUR TRIALS AND TRIBULATIONS. ATTITUDE IS ALL, SO CULTIVATE THE ABILITY TO LET GO OF ALL YOUR THOUGHTS AND PREOCCUPATIONS AND PUT THEM ON HOLD FOR A FEW MOMENTS.

- SIT OR LIE QUIETLY AND COMFORTABLY AND AS YOU RELAX, BEGIN TO OBSERVE YOUR BREATHING. DON'T TRY TO ALTER IT IN ANY WAY, JUST BECOME AWARE OF IT.
- FEEL THE RISE AND FALL OF YOUR ABDOMEN AS YOU BREATHE IN AND OUT.
- NOTICE THE PASSAGE OF YOUR BREATH; CAN YOU FEEL IT AS IT ENTERS YOUR NOSTRILS?
- WATCH THE WAYS YOUR BODY RESPONDS TO YOUR INCOMING BREATH AND OUTGOING BREATH.

- As your breathing becomes more regular and begins to slow down your mind will start to relax and become more peaceful.
- Stay in this quiet space for a while and enjoy the peace and stillness.

Let this new sense of relaxation stay with you and deepen your appreciation of your everyday moments. In this state you will develop a lighter approach to life; issues will feel less serious and your sense of humour will shine through.

Don't forget to enjoy the precious moments of your life; don't let anything take away your sense of peace, joy, fun and happiness.

Having fun means ...

- **Finding time for leisure activities.** If this feels impossible then take a long hard look at your beliefs about the value of enjoyment in life. Perhaps, deep down you believe that it would be selfish to indulge in delightful activities. Check out your long-held beliefs about having fun by completing the following statement:

  Fun is . . . .

If you discover an inner reluctance to get in touch with your sense of humour try using the following affirmations:

My life is full of fun
I am a pleasure seeker
Laughter is good for me

I enjoy life every day
Nothing stands in the way of my happiness
I deserve to have fun

- **Being able to relax, even when the going gets tough.** Unhappy people usually seem surprised and unprepared when negativity strikes; they are floored and upset and immediately lose their spirit. Happy people will bounce back because they can depend on their inner resilience; they accept that things are not always easy and they have a contingency plan for dealing with stress. So be prepared to cultivate your bouncing-back qualities. You can do this by developing some simple and effective relaxation techniques such as: yoga; t'ai chi; walking; meeting up with friends; a cycle ride; meditation; swimming; dancing . . . Don't sit in a pit of negativity and let life get you down, do something that will move and change your energy. Help yourself through difficult times by doing something that you know will alter your tense state. I find a simple walk in the countryside can totally change my outlook on things. The relaxation techniques that work best are usually very simple and easy to do.

- **Not caring what others think.** Some people are inhibited by the idea of having fun because they are afraid that they might look foolish or weak in the eyes of others. Unhappiness is often accompanied by an overwhelming preoccupation with the opinion of other people. But it's always well worth remembering that everyone else is usually far too self-involved to be spending time looking at you and judging your behaviour. If you are struggling to have fun, just check if you are trying to fulfil someone else's expectations. Are you doing your own thing or just jumping through the hoops? And if you are not being true to yourself then why is this? Perhaps it's time to be yourself and to acknowledge what really makes *you* happy and to do much more of it. Let your inner pleasure lover see the light of day and you will immediately notice the effect this has on your social life; fun-filled people are amazingly attractive to others.

- **Valuing the importance of a joyful attitude.** Robert Louis Stevenson said that: 'There is no duty we so much underrate as the duty of being happy. By being happy we sow anonymous benefits upon the world.' Bear these wise words in mind whenever you question your right to have a fun-filled and enjoyable life. We spread positivity and hope to others by simply being happy. Smiling and laughing are infectious and so are moaning and blaming. It's sometimes hard to imagine how a kind word and gesture can have far-reaching effects, but they do; when we uplift the spirit of others this positive vibration is passed on down the line. And once we know how to spread our happiness about we have a duty to ourselves and to others to continue to do this. Of course, what goes around comes around and so the joy givers become even happier. Take having fun seriously!

- **Being more accepting of yourself and others.** Having fun often requires the company of others, and research shows that laughter is thirty times more likely to occur in a group situation than a solitary one. People with a good social life are those who are able to accept people for who they are rather than being critical and judgemental. And those who find it difficult to socialise are often people who are very hard on themselves and have high expectations of others. A study at the University of Illinois in 2002 demonstrated that the most important characteristics shared by the 10 per cent of students with the highest levels of happiness and the fewest signs of depression were their strong ties to friends and family and their commitment to spending time with them. If your social life needs revitalising it might be time to get out and about and mix with others.

ACTIVITY: BECOMING A PLEASURE SEEKER

Simple pleasures are fun and increase our levels of happiness. Make a list of your top ten pleasures.

Here are a few suggestions to get you started

Cooking a special meal for a loved one.

Visiting a friend.

Eating something delicious.

Taking a walk in the park.

Listening to a favourite piece of music.

Reading a great novel.

Going to the theatre.

Taking part in a team game.

Learning a new language.

Browsing in a bookshop.

Taking an art class.

Beginning a new hobby.

DOING SOMETHING FOR SOMEONE ELSE.

HAVING AN ALLOTMENT.

RIDING YOUR BIKE.

SPENDING TIME WITH CHILDREN.

JOINING AN EXERCISE CLASS.

TAKING A CREATIVE WRITING COURSE.

PLAYING SCRABBLE.

BAKING A CHOCOLATE CAKE AND EATING SOME!

WATCHING A FAVOURITE MOVIE.

SITTING IN A COFFEE SHOP, PEOPLE WATCHING.

AND NOW CHOOSE ONE OF YOUR TOP TEN PLEASURES TO ENJOY TODAY. CHOOSE ANOTHER ONE TOMORROW. MAKE SURE THAT YOU DO SOMETHING *JUST FOR PLEASURE* EVERY DAY.

Life can be an exciting adventure every single day

When my granddaughter comes to stay my life takes on many different aspects; the world slows down and every detail starts to become more meaningful and important. She asks so many questions about things that I take for granted and I find myself looking at the world in a fresh, new way. Crayons, felt tips, coloured paper and scissors suddenly fascinate me again and soon we are making dancing dolls and collages galore; the whole house starts to burst with creativity. The dining-room table becomes a permanent workshop space and even my grown-up sons get busy turning out such things as origami swans and gnashers (monster mouths that gobble up little girls!). A walk in the park becomes a massive adventure filled with all manner of incidents with dogs and strangers; it seems that everyone wants to stop and chat when Alaska is skipping along next to me.

Although you are grown-up your inner child is still alive and well and hoping for some fun. Given half a chance even the most grumpily serious adult can enjoy plasticine, play dough and paints or a visit to a theme park or fair. If you haven't any children of your own borrow a godchild, a niece or nephew or a friend's child for the afternoon and go and do something childish. Tap into the child within you and you will rediscover many forgotten delights; happy grown-ups are those who remember that life can be an exciting adventure every single day.

Hazel's story

Hazel said that she felt 'depressed and negative' when she began her first coaching session with me. She was in her mid-thirties and worked as an accountant for a large firm. Her long-term partner was talking about them having a child together and she was struggling with the idea. She described herself as a serious person who had worked hard to climb the career ladder, she often stayed late at the office and she and her partner, Sean, spent very little time together. When I asked her about leisure activities and hobbies she smiled ruefully and said that she really couldn't afford the time for anything other than work. She admitted that Sean had been trying to encourage her to take some time out and even cut down her hours so that they could do more together and maybe start a family but Hazel said that this prospect 'terrified' her. Sean was beginning to question her commitment to him and she felt challenged by him and worried about the future.

We talked a bit about Hazel's life as a child and she told me that her father was a Methodist minister and her upbringing had been pretty austere. When I asked her to tell me about her happy childhood memories she said she hadn't got any because she always had to be responsible. She was the eldest of five and spent most of her time helping her mother with her siblings. Hazel was a straight A student at the local grammar school and went on to achieve a First Class degree in economics and accountancy. She then went to work in a nearby firm (where she had met Sean) and had been there ever since.

I asked her how she felt about committing herself to more time with Sean and to the possibility of having a child. She said that it all sounded too problematic and tiring. We discussed what it had been like for her to carry the responsibility of caring for her brothers and sisters and she said that it had put her off having any children of her own.

At the next session she told me that she had talked to Sean about what we had discussed and that he was suggesting that they went away on a relaxing holiday for a couple of weeks so that they could just spend some time together. Hazel admitted that she was a bit of a workaholic and the prospect of taking two weeks off was daunting. This would be the first time in three years that they had gone on holiday together. But she decided to go and when she came back she was quite different. She was bubbling with excitement as she told me how they had been water-skiing and scuba diving and how she had loved the laid-back atmosphere of the Caribbean. She said that Sean and her had decided to move out of the town and into a village nearby so that they could slow down their pace but still have easy access to work. They had spent a lot of time just relaxing and talking about their possible future, and Sean had asked Hazel to marry him. Somehow Hazel had managed to let the fun back into her life and she said that she felt like a totally different woman and so much more relaxed; she was already planning her wedding. She was thrilled to discover that she could enjoy herself and let her hair down and she was even talking about the possibility of being a mum.

It can be only too easy to get stuck in a comfortable routine that seems to offer a feeling of security and control, but when we do this the spontaneity and excitement can go from our life. Sometimes having fun can require a bit of effort on our part; we need to find the time and the inclination, but it's always worth it when we do. Don't forget that the child inside you is raring to break out a bit and let her hair down, so give her a chance and you will discover that life can be fascinating, interesting, creative and happy!

CHANGE ONE THING

CULTIVATE YOUR INNER SMILE

YOUR INNER SMILE COMES FROM A SENSE OF PEACE AND TRANQUILLITY; IT'S A FEELING THAT ALL IS RIGHT WITH THE WORLD. AND OF COURSE YOUR INNER SMILE NATURALLY TURNS INTO AN OUTWARD SMILE.

- TAP INTO YOUR INNER FEELINGS AS YOU GO ABOUT YOUR DAY.

- NOTICE WHEN YOU EXPERIENCE THIS FEELING THAT EVERYTHING IS OK. RECOGNISE THAT YOU ARE SMILING INSIDE AND ENJOY YOUR FEELINGS OF CONTENTMENT.

Develop the gratitude habit

The more we complain the worse we feel and we open the door to despondency and misery every time we fail to appreciate the wonderful gift of life. Throughout this book we have seen again and again how our habitual responses can increase or decrease our levels of happiness and fun. We know that if we focus on the negative aspects of daily life then we will easily slip into the cycle of unhappiness and that this only leads to further depression. And how can we enjoy the doughnut if we can only ever see the hole?

Gratitude research is part of the developing science of positive psychology and seeks to test the value of counting one's blessings. Michael McCullough, psychology professor at the University of Miami, has conducted the most widely cited study on gratitude. He says that, 'Grateful people are happier, more optimistic, more satisfied with their lives . . . They are more empathetic toward others.' All the scientific evidence demonstrates that the gratitude habit is very good for us. It brings fun and laughter into our lives and helps us to withstand everyday disappointments and setbacks. So why not try your own bit of research now? Take a moment to consider everything that you have that you feel grateful for at the moment; nothing is too small to consider. You may like to develop this habit so that you make a regular daily point of counting your blessings. Some people write their gratitude list before they go to sleep each night and many clients tell me that they have been greatly uplifted by doing this. You might just look out of the window now and take a moment to appreciate the clouds in the sky, the leaves on a tree, and your feelings of gratitude.

Once you start to count your blessings a wonderful, magical process begins as you open your heart in thankfulness for the miracle of your life. And the more you start to appreciate what you have the more positive and optimistic and fun-filled your days will become. As Yoko Ono says, 'Count your blessings and enjoy every minute of life.'

REFRESH AND RENEW

WE ALL WANT TO BE LOVED AND APPRECIATED

TAKE A MOMENT TO CONTEMPLATE THIS THOUGHT. WE ARE AT OUR BEST WHEN WE FEEL NEEDED AND APPRECIATED AND THESE FEELINGS MUST BEGIN INSIDE US. ONCE WE START LOOKING OUTSIDE OURSELVES FOR APPROVAL WE WILL ALWAYS FEEL LET DOWN. BUT WHEN WE FEEL THAT INNER LOVE FOR OURSELVES THEN OTHERS WILL REFLECT THAT BACK TO US.

THE MORE YOU CAN APPRECIATE YOURSELF THE MORE OTHERS WILL APPRECIATE YOU.

- SIT QUIETLY, CLOSE YOUR EYES AND IMAGINE THAT YOUR HEART IS FULL OF LOVE.

- IMAGINE A BEAUTIFUL BRIGHTNESS ENTERING EVERY CELL OF YOUR BODY AND FILLING YOU WITH JOY AND PEACE.

- REST IN THIS BEAUTIFUL GLOW FOR A WHILE AND KNOW THAT YOU ARE LOVED AND APPRECIATED AND THAT YOU ARE FABULOUS!

- WHEN YOU OPEN YOUR EYES TRY TAKING THIS WARM GLOW WITH YOU OUT INTO THE WORLD. YES, YOU ARE TRULY AMAZING!

Day 8 TODAY'S HAPPINESS ROUNDUP

Once more it's time to reflect on your day. Circle your score and fill out the sections in your journal.

MY HAPPINESS SCORE FOR THE DAY

TOTALLY   FABULOUS
FED-UP

1   2   3   4   5   6   7   8   9   10

Most significant event of the day

....

....

My main concern of the day

....

....

What can I do about this, if anything?

....

....

Most useful happiness strategies today

....

....

What went well today

....

....

Three things that made me smile today

....

....

As before, take a few moments to make a note of anything that made a particular impact on you today.

Final reflections

- You can't be unhappy when you are having fun.
- When life gets serious just check how important the issue is. Does it really matter?
- Finding the time to have some fun will make all the difference to the quality of your life.
- The child inside you is longing for some fun and excitement.
- Counting your blessings will always remind you that you have so much to be grateful for.

Day 9

Go for Your Dreams

Without leaps of the imagination, or dreaming,
we lose the excitement of possibilities. Dreaming,
after all is a form of planning.

GLORIA STEINEM

Twenty years from now you will be more
disappointed by the things that you didn't do than
by the ones you did do. So throw off the bowlines.
Sail away from the safe harbour. Catch the trade
winds in your sails. Explore. Dream. Discover.

MARK TWAIN

Unhappiness is usually a sign that our old ways of dealing with situations are no longer working for us; change is afoot and we need to act appropriately. But of course when things are difficult that familiar and cosy harbour will feel like the very safest place to stay.

Throughout this book we have seen that happy people have a set of attitudes and responses that mark them out from their more pessimistic counterparts. An optimistic and hopeful view leads to excitement at the prospect of change and these positive qualities make it possible for us to face our future with confidence and flexibility. However, although we might know that it's time to move on, our goals may lack clarity and we may lack motivation. And this is where good life coaching comes into its own. It provides a useful structure for those who know that they need to alter something in their lives but aren't quite sure where to start; it lays down some simple ground rules and encourages action! Today is your chance to apply the principles of life coaching to any area of your life where you would like to make changes.

When we considered Professor Seligman's suggested three paths to happiness (Day 5, page 111) it became clear that long-lasting contentment depends upon the extent to which we feel engaged with our everyday life and committed to our outcomes. In other words, we experience a sense of meaning and purpose when we know what we want to accomplish and we are motivated to achieve our goals. It is interesting to note that there have been a number of psychologists (including the great Carl Jung) who have found that many of their clients did not suffer from psychosis or neurosis, but from aimlessness and meaninglessness.

Happy people are motivated people and unhappy people lack this driving force. If you are low in energy and focus at the moment you will feel miserable and it will be hard to put a smile on your face because a lack of direction only serves to increase our levels of unhappiness. But it can be quite easy to break this negative cycle by simply making a decision to take some action. And positive action is a direct way to confront apathy, discontentment and negativity. It may well be time for you to catch those trade winds in your sails and go on to explore and discover something fresh and new by going for your dreams.

CHANGE ONE THING

BY TAKING POSITIVE ACTION

- CONSIDER ANY ASPECT OF YOUR LIFE THAT YOU WOULD LIKE TO CHANGE.

- Now develop this notion by giving it more focus. You can do this by writing down exactly what you would like to happen.

- What would you have to believe about yourself in order for you to make your outcome come about?

- Imagine that you have all the qualities you need to take charge and to bring about the changes you desire.

- Visualise yourself implementing the changes. See your successful outcome and experience the new energy it brings.

- Stay with this positive energy while you consider the next step that you would need to take to bring your outcome nearer.

- Commit yourself to the next step by writing a simple plan of action.

- When will you take the next step? Give yourself a realistic deadline.

- Stick to your deadline. You will be amazed to discover that the next step that you need to take will become very clear and obvious.

And this is the way that positive action works: each small step leading to the next.

Developing the confidence to go for your goals

You might have a clear vision of your preferred future and know the steps you need to take but still be unable to commit yourself to an action plan. If a lack of confidence stops you moving forward then you need to face your doubts head-on and check how realistic they are. When we are thrashing around in self-doubt we are often inclined to believe that we lack the necessary confidence to do whatever it is we are being called to do. But confidence is a quality that is often bestowed on us *after* we have taken what feels like a risky step. By definition, moving out of a comfort zone is bound to feel uncomfortable, but if you can take your courage in both hands and believe in yourself (in spite of your fears) the personal rewards are huge. As soon as you take that leap of faith your confidence immediately rises; yes, you *did* go for it and this in itself increases your self-belief. The more you are prepared to act on your own behalf the more you will trust yourself to be able to make good choices and clear decisions. In the immortal words of Eleanor Roosevelt: 'You gain strength, courage, and confidence by every experience in which you really stop to look fear in the face. You must do the thing which you think you cannot do.'

Our self-limiting thoughts are usually based in old negative beliefs that have very little basis in reality. But here's the thing: we can never achieve anything unless we can believe that it is possible for us. For example, if I don't believe that I can get that great promotion then I probably won't even bother to apply for it. And even if I do my doubts will affect the quality of my application and interview. Lack of self-belief is as obvious as a measles rash. So decide not to indulge yourself in beliefs about what you can't do and instead focus on what you can do. Stop waiting for confidence to appear in your life and start to develop it by thinking and acting positively. Confident and courageous people are self-starters who have acquired these personal qualities by following their dreams and overcoming failures and disappointments by bouncing back over and over again.

How to be a self-starter

Ask yourself the following questions and find out if you have what it takes to go for your goals.

Where do I want to be in five years' time?

If you carry on doing what you are doing will you have reached your outcome? Are you actively working towards that future now? Such questions are sometimes all it takes to kick-start us into action.

What do I need to believe about myself before I can go for my dreams?

When we put our fabulous plans on hold for too long we become dispirited, demotivated, unenthusiastic and generally depressed. If you are feeling disappointed by life then this a sign that you are not doing what you are here to do. Those negative self-beliefs will always keep you down so *stop indulging them*. Believe the very best about yourself and you will develop all the confidence you need to move forward.

Where have I been successful in the past?

We all have a habit of moving goalposts. In other words, as soon as we have achieved something we busily rush on to the next thing without celebrating our success. Look back at your significant achievements and let them remind you of your inner strength and your ability to see things through. You did it then and you can do it now!

How can I maintain my motivation?

It's easy to get enthusiastic at the beginning of a project when we are full of exciting ideas. But then, when we need to activate our plans and get down to the practical details, our wonderful project might just feel like a lot of hard work. A great way to stay motivated is to keep taking a short-term view. Don't keep looking at the long-term goal or you will get impatient and lose interest. Break down your action plan into manageable bite-sized chunks so that you are always achieving something. And keep patting yourself on the back each time you take a new step, however small it might be.

Do I really love my goal?

I know that we have looked at this issue before but it is such an important subject. We change, circumstances alter and goals sometimes need to be revised. Keep checking your commitment to your outcome and if you feel your interest waning consider why this might be. Be warned: if you don't love your goal then you are unlikely to achieve it.

When did I last demonstrate my ability to bounce back?

Recognise your inner strength and powers of resilience by casting your mind back to past challenges. Consider the last time you faced a major setback. How did you respond to the situation and how did you cope with any difficult feelings? You see, you have bounced back before and so you know that you have all the resilience you need. Use this technique whenever you doubt your strength of spirit.

Do I act confidently?

If you are taking a step that looks like a risk then you might not feel very confident, but you can boost your positive power by behaving confidently. If you act timidly then you will lose all self-belief and others will pick up on your insecurity. So bravely step forward, take a deep breath, adopt good posture, put on a happy face and then just do what has to be done. Act confidently and you will feel and think confidently.

How will I know the right steps to take?

If you have made a sensible action plan then one step will inevitably lead to the next. But being a successful self-starter is not only about what you *do,* it also depends upon your ability to tap into your gut feelings. Trust your instincts before you make a decision and go with what feels right for you.

H A P P I N E S S   T I P

TAKE GOOD CARE OF YOURSELF

LIFE CAN BE A CHALLENGE, THERE'S NO DOUBT ABOUT IT. HOWEVER HARD WE WORK ON MAINTAINING OUR POSITIVITY THERE WILL BE TIMES WHEN WE FEEL UNDULY STRESSED; THIS IS QUITE NATURAL. BEGIN TO RECOGNISE THOSE MOMENTS WHEN YOU FEEL OVERLOADED AND DO SOMETHING TO BRING BACK YOUR FEELINGS OF WELLBEING. KNOW WHEN YOU ARE ABOUT TO GO UNDER AND ADMIT THAT IT'S TIME FOR YOU TO STOP.

- TAKE SOME TIME OUT WHEREVER YOU ARE. EVEN IF YOU ARE AT WORK YOU CAN TAKE A MOMENT TO SLOW DOWN AND GET THINGS BACK INTO PERSPECTIVE.

- BREAK A NEGATIVE CYCLE BY DOING SOMETHING JUST FOR YOU; DEMONSTRATE TO YOURSELF THAT YOU ARE WORTH IT!

- TAKE A WALK, A BATH, A SWIM; MOVE YOUR BODY IN SOME WAY AND YOU WILL NATURALLY LIFT YOUR MOOD.

ALWAYS REMEMBER THAT YOU ARE PURSUING YOUR GOALS BECAUSE YOU THINK THAT THEY WILL MAKE YOU HAPPY. EVERY NOW AND AGAIN STOP AND CHECK THAT THE OUTCOME IS WORTH THE PRICE YOU ARE PAYING.

Have no fear

While I was writing this chapter, record-breaking yachts-woman Dee Caffari returned from her heroic journey to become the first woman to circumnavigate the globe 29,000 miles, solo and non-stop the 'wrong way' around the planet, against the forces of the earth's rotation and winds.

Although your goals may not be of such epic proportions the principles required for your success will be the same. You will need to know exactly what you are aiming for and you will have to do all the necessary groundwork and preparation. Obviously your motivation and determination must be high and you will have to have a positive and realistic notion of what is possible for you to achieve. The mental tests will also be similar: the biggest challenge to your success will lie in your own self-belief and your ability to maintain a 'can-do' approach in the face of adversity. In an interview with the *Daily Telegraph* newspaper Dee said that her motto is: 'If you want to go and do it, do it. Have no fear.' She also admitted that the toughest part of her sporting challenges was her fear of failure. We all face that fear when we embark on something that we have set our heart upon but go-getters feel it *and just keep going*.

Throughout her journey Dee was in contact with her personal coach, Harry Spedding, who posted news of her on his website. When she reached the halfway point Harry wrote that she entered '. . . one of the hardest battles so far', when she had to '. . . deal emotionally with the extent of the voyage still ahead of her'. He said, 'At the moment, it is sheer determination and a healthy dose of bloody mindedness that is keeping her going.'

Anyone who has embarked on achieving a long-term goal will know just how it feels to have come so far along the path and yet to still have so much further to go; it can be emotionally difficult to keep focused and determined and it may be very tempting to give up. But it is at this point where sheer guts and determination and a desire to succeed can give us the energy and enthusiasm to take us through and beyond this difficult phase. I once had a client who was trying to lose four stones in weight and she contacted me after she had lost the first two stones. Her battle was purely psychological; she knew exactly what she needed to do to lose the weight but her resolve was weakening. She used our coaching sessions to inspire and motivate her and also she knew that she would have to tell me if she didn't stick to her regime. Eventually she lost the weight but meanwhile she had started training for a new career and her life was really taking off. I have often noticed how clients use the inner strengths they acquire when they successfully achieve one goal to go on to make positive changes in other parts of their life. When you can overcome your fears you can achieve your dreams; have no fear!

Choose the goals that will bring you happiness

Hungarian psychologist Mihaly Csikszentmihalyi conducted a worldwide study into the phenomenon of optimal experience. In his book *Flow* he writes that: 'While happiness is sought for its own sake, every other goal – health, beauty, money or power – is valued only because we expect that it will make us happy.' Mihaly's book explores people's experiences of feeling fully alive and he identifies a class of 'flow activities' as being those that completely absorb and engage the participants.

Think back to any occasion when you were deeply immersed in something and time seemed to stand still; you were in the zone! When we are involved in any pursuit that creates flow activity, our body and mind work harmoniously together and we feel focused, motivated and confident. But we don't have to be athletes or artists to experience the benefits of being in the zone. This optimal experience is something that we can make happen by ensuring that we restructure our activities so that we have clear, attainable and happy-making goals. Csikszentmihalyi used the term flow because many of his interviewees had used it to describe how it felt to be on top form ('I was carried along by the flow'). He goes on to say that those who attained flow developed a stronger, more confident self because they had invested in goals that they themselves had chosen to pursue.

Karen's story

Karen, 44, was a teacher at a well-known independent school for girls when her husband, John, took early retirement. At our first session she told me that she was fed-up with her life and work and felt a lot of resentment for her husband and that she was considering leaving him. But as we talked over the situation it became more and more obvious that although she was blaming her relationship for her unhappiness her dissatisfaction was really with herself and her own lack of motivation and interest in life.

She had worked at the school for twenty-two years and had gone there as soon as she had finished her training. Karen said that she had often wanted to leave and do something 'a bit more adventurous' but that she felt so institutionalised that she was afraid that she wasn't equipped to enter what she called 'the real world'. She had gone into teaching because a career's advisor had suggested it when she was seventeen. At that time it had seemed a safe option. After graduating in History at Durham University she went on to do a Postgraduate Certificate in Education and then began her job. Karen admitted that she had never felt a natural vocation for teaching but her job had fitted in well when she had her two children and somehow the years had passed by and now here she was, aged forty-four and longing to start something new.

It's not hard to see that Karen's unhappiness was linked with a real lack of engagement and interest in her job but when I suggested a change of career she said that she felt unable to make any move in a new direction. Eventually she decided to discuss things with John (who knew nothing about how she was feeling) and the next time we spoke she was full of new plans. It seemed that John had also been looking for something new and interesting to get his teeth into and so they had decided to sell their house and move to Somerset to open a small hotel in the Quantocks (an area that they both loved). And that was that! Karen sounded invigorated by the new challenge ahead and she and John had a shared goal that excited them both.

If you are feeling flat and demotivated just take another look at where you are going and why. It might be that you have stopped enjoying flow activities because you are no longer pursuing a goal that delights you. Sometimes we just get sidetracked into taking an easy option or following a dream that belongs to someone else (perhaps even just doing what a career's advisor suggested many years ago). Stop now and ask yourself when you last felt in top form and carried along by the flow. You might need to create some new, vibrant goals that really express what you would love to achieve. Happy people choose goals that will make them even happier!

ACTIVITY: MAKING SURE MY GOALS ARE SMART *

IF YOU WANT TO CONVERT YOUR DREAMS INTO REALITY THEN YOU MUST BE SURE THAT YOU KNOW EXACTLY WHAT YOU ARE GOING FOR; YOU NEED TO NAME YOUR GOAL AND THEN MAKE SURE THAT IT IS SMART.

SPECIFIC: CLARIFY YOUR GOAL; WHAT *EXACTLY* DO YOU WANT?

MEASURABLE: QUANTIFY YOUR GOAL IN SOME WAY SO THAT YOU CAN EVALUATE YOUR PROGRESS.

ATTRACTIVE:	I**F YOU LOVE YOUR GOAL YOU WILL ACHIEVE IT AND IF YOU DON'T THEN YOU WON'T BE ABLE TO SUSTAIN THE NECESSARY MOTIVATION.**
REALISTIC:	Y**OU MUST KNOW IN YOUR HEART OF HEARTS THAT YOU CAN ACHIEVE YOUR GOAL. D**ON'T **SET IT TOO HIGH OR YOU WILL GET DISCOURAGED. B**UT DON'T SET IT TOO LOW **EITHER, BECAUSE YOU NEED TO STRETCH YOURSELF.**
TIME-FRAMED:	S**PECIFY A TIME FOR YOU TO ACHIEVE EACH STEP ALONG THE WAY. R**EALISTIC DEADLINES **WILL DO WONDERS FOR YOUR MOTIVATION.**

* A**DAPTED FROM MY BOOK,** *W**EEKEND** C**ONFIDENCE** C**OACH.***

Are you feeling perfectly unhappy?

In a recent workshop on success we were discussing the reasons why we might choose to sabotage our goals; in other words, why we may be afraid to be successful. One man said that he feared success because he thought that once he had achieved a goal he would have to maintain that level of accomplishment, and the possibility of the pressure involved made him feel unhappy. Others said that they felt that high self-expectations could lead to disappointment and misery rather than to greater achievement and happiness. This then developed into a discussion about perfectionism.

It seems that all this talk of goal-getting and going for dreams can bring out the very worst in some people.

Perfectionists can easily create a no-win/no-happiness situation when they set out to achieve their goals by: striving to reach the ideal; never settling for anything that is less than perfect; never accepting mistakes; expecting the highest of standards from everyone else and never being able to be 'good enough' to feel successful.

Although you might not be a perfectionist it is worth considering any tendencies you might have in this direction as they would certainly have a negative influence on your happiness levels. It is so easy to sabotage our plans by being overcritical of our endeavours. We all have a strong inner critical voice that is busy telling us how we should or must do something or how we are getting too big for our boots or that we don't deserve to achieve our goals. This voice often gets quite loud as we approach the realisation of our dreams. If you lose self-belief then just check on whether you are listening to this inner critical voice.

- Tell yourself that you are doing well and that you are good enough just the way you are.
- Check that you are not expecting perfection and be able to recognise when you have done a 'good enough' job. Remember that no one is perfect and that if you become obsessive about the flawlessness of any project you will never achieve success. Perfectionism and self-criticism will keep you in an unhappy state of indecision and irresolution and you will fail to reach your dreams.
- Accept your imperfections and admire your stamina as you overcome your doubts and move happily towards the fulfilment of your goals.

As writer Ursula K. Le Guin poetically reminds us: 'It is good to have an end to journey toward, but it is the journey that matters in the end.'

CHANGE ONE THING

BY CREATING AN INNER AND OUTER ACTION PLAN

SOME OF US ARE ACTION ORIENTED AND FIND IT EASY TO TAKE PRACTICAL STEPS TOWARDS OUR OUTCOMES. AND SOME OF US ARE MORE INNER DIRECTED AND FIND IT EASIER TO VISUALISE AND AFFIRM OUR GOALS. BUT THE KEY TO SUCCESS LIES IN COMBINING THESE TWO APPROACHES.

- RECOGNISE IF YOU ARE INCLINED TO USE AN ASSERTIVE GO-GETTING APPROACH OR A MORE IMAGINATIVE AND INSPIRED STYLE. YOU WILL PROBABLY BE INCLINED TO FAVOUR ONE METHOD MORE THAN THE OTHER.

- IF YOU ARE GOOD AT VISUALISING AND IMAGINING YOUR OUTCOME BUT FIND IT HARDER TO ACTUALLY GET GOING THEN YOU NEED TO BALANCE YOUR ENERGY. KEEP DOING THE INNER WORK BUT MATCH IT WITH REAL LIFE ACTIVITY. GET OUT THERE AND MAKE THE MOVES YOU NEED TO MAKE OR YOUR GLORIOUS DREAMS WILL REMAIN A FIGMENT OF YOUR IMAGINATION.

- IF YOU ARE PROACTIVE BUT NOT SO GOOD AT VISUALISING YOUR OUTCOMES AND MAKING SUPPORTIVE AFFIRMATIONS THEN YOU NEED TO START PRACTISING THESE MORE INNER-DIRECTED ACTIVITIES.

> • WHEN WE ARE MAKING OUR DREAMS COME TRUE WE ARE
> INVOLVED IN A CREATIVE ACT THAT INVOLVES WORKING
> WITH BOTH AN INNER AND AN OUTER ACTION PLAN. IF
> YOU GET THESE IN BALANCE THEN YOUR CHANCES OF
> SUCCESS INCREASE DRAMATICALLY.

Reassessing your Happiness Audit

Your day-to-day happiness depends upon the quality of your moments: are you making the most of your time, having fun and enjoying yourself or are you spending your precious hours involved in joyless activities?

Take another look at the Happiness Audit that you created on Day 2. What did you learn from your Happiness Rating Table? Which areas of your life bring you happiness and where would you like to make changes? Are you working towards fulfilling your dreams or are you just marking time? Perhaps you can use the information you gained from your audit to help you to identify some exciting new paths to take. Bear in mind all that we have discovered about the importance of creating meaningful goals that bring us pleasure. And the more 'flow activities' we enjoy the happier we will be, so ensure that you make time to incorporate all the things you love to do.

Here are two examples of how we can translate the findings of our audit to create new, SMART and happy-making goals.

Example 1: You spend 8 hours a day in a job that you don't enjoy; your happiness score for work is 3. Obviously it's time for a change. Consider all your options and choose the best one. What would you love to do? What is stopping you? If you need to retrain then investigate how you can set about this. If you would like to be self-employed and you have a good business idea then focus on getting this off the ground (keep the day job until you know your business can support you). Do you need any advice: business/financial/career/educational . . . ? If so then take it.

Clients often find it hard to clarify their goals, so if you feel like this just go back to that concept of 'flow activities'. What is it that excites and delights you so much? When are you in the zone? I had a client who was unhappy working for an advertising agency and just loved working out and was passionate about health and fitness. She created an action plan and made sure that her goals were SMART. Eventually she retrained as a personal fitness coach and now runs her own consultancy. You *can* earn money doing something that you love.

Example 2: You scored 2 in your relationship category. What can you do about this? Perhaps there are some things that need to be said. Why aren't you saying them? How long can you continue feeling so unhappy? Ask yourself what you want from this relationship. Get things down on paper and write some relationship goals. Your goal might be to improve communication between the two of you so you make it **specific** by writing: *I want us to communicate well with each other.* You could **measure** your progress by becoming aware of whether or not he is as eager as you to improve your relationship: is he showing signs of reciprocating? Your goal is **attractive** because you love your partner and so you are highly motivated. And the goal is **realistic** because you have been together for two happy years and it's only in the last three months that it has started to go downhill. You have given it a **time-frame** by deciding to make the relationship your main focus for the next month and then if nothing has improved you will make a clear decision about whether it is worth continuing.

Sometimes we have to make way for our dreams by clearing up the debris that is blocking our path. If your goal is to have a great relationship with a compatible man and you find yourself continually in poor relationships, then it might be necessary for you to pull back and reassess your situation. You deserve to have a wonderful and loving relationship so make sure you don't settle for anything less!

REFRESH AND RENEW

YOUR HEART'S DESIRE

FIND A COMFORTABLE AND UNDISTURBED SPOT. SIT BACK AND RELAX.

- AS YOUR BREATHING BEGINS TO SLOW DOWN AND YOU FEEL YOURSELF UNWINDING, LET YOUR EYES GENTLY CLOSE.

- TAKE A FEW MOMENTS TO PEACEFULLY RELAX.

- AND THEN, IN YOUR MIND'S EYE SEE A BIG, EMPTY WHITE CINEMA SCREEN IN FRONT OF YOU.

- YOU CAN NOW SEE A MOVIE PICTURE OF ANYTHING THAT YOU WOULD LOVE TO CREATE IN YOUR REAL LIFE.

- SEE YOURSELF ON SCREEN REACHING YOUR VERY BEST AND

LIVING YOUR HEART'S DESIRE. FEEL HOW WONDERFUL IT
WOULD BE TO BE REACHING YOUR FULL POTENTIAL.
EXPERIENCE ALL THE FEELINGS THAT THIS BRINGS.

- REFLECT UPON WHATEVER YOU SAW ON THE SCREEN.
  WHAT IS IT THAT YOU WOULD LOVE TO DO?

- WHAT WOULD YOU HAVE TO BELIEVE ABOUT YOURSELF
  IN ORDER TO MAKE THIS VISUALISATION COME TRUE?

- START TO BELIEVE THIS NOW.

Day 9 TODAY'S HAPPINESS ROUNDUP

It is time to reflect on your day. Circle your score and fill out
the sections in your journal.

MY HAPPINESS SCORE FOR THE DAY

TOTALLY   FABULOUS
FED-UP
   1   2   3   4   5   6   7   8   9   10

Most significant event of the day

....

....

My main concern of the day

....

....

What can I do about this, if anything?

....

....

Most useful happiness strategies today

....

....

What went well today

....

....

Three things that made me smile today

....

....

As before, take a few moments to make a note of anything that made a particular impact on you today.

Final reflections

- Positive action is one of the most powerful antidotes to apathy, discontent and negativity.
- Confidence is a quality that is often bestowed on us *after* we have taken what feels like a risky step.
- When you can overcome your fears you can achieve your dreams; have no fear!
- Check that you are not expecting perfection and be able to recognise when you have done a 'good enough' job.
- Sometimes we have to make way for our dreams by clearing up the debris that is blocking our path.

Happy Ever After

If we are brave enough to allow even a small amount of uncertainty into our lives, we have more chance of discovering new avenues of satisfaction and happiness. You have to speculate to accumulate.

NOEL EDMONDS

To date I have only ever written happy endings.
Having lived with my characters for several months
before I write their particular endings I have always
felt compelled to give them at least a Happily Near
Future (if not a Happy Ever After). I think my
readers deserve happy endings; there's enough
grimness to deal with without my adding to it.
Yet if Anna and Vronsky or Scarlett and Rhett had
lived happily-ever-after we would have forgotten them.
Happiness doesn't have the cachet and miserable
nobility of tragedy, at least not in literature. In
real life I'm rather keen on it.

ADELE PARKS

'. . . and they all lived happily ever after'. Ah, that has such a comforting ring to it, doesn't it? As a child I remember listening to my father reading me my favourite fairy stories and all the while I would be patiently waiting for that magical ending, when everything would be happily resolved as I had known it would all along. Now I read to my granddaughter and she listens in that same contented way for a joyful resolution. When true love prevails and goodness triumphs over evil we feel an inherent sense of 'rightness'; all is well with the world. And in real life which of us would ever choose the 'nobility of tragedy' over the delight of happiness?

Novelist Adele Parks thinks her readers deserve happy endings and I think that you do too. So, on this last day we will be looking at how you can create a happy ever after scenario for yourself; today you can set the scene for every day that follows.

Fast Track to Happiness has examined some recurring fundamental themes, and perhaps the most important one is the idea that happiness is an inside job. By this I mean that our state of mind dictates our mood and that by using various tactics and techniques we can overcome a negative disposition. Once we can accept that life is not always easy, and that we are all bound to face various trials and tribulations, then we can adopt a realistic attitude to our pursuit of personal happiness.

To maintain an upbeat and decisive attitude we certainly need to stick with the strategies that we know will work for us, and the last nine days of the Happiness Programme will have highlighted everything you need to know in order to create your very own Happiness Action Plan. As you look through your journal you will discover that some of the tips uplifted your spirits more than others.

Perhaps you were inclined to submit to feeling pessimistic and now need to concentrate on learning a more optimistic approach. Or if you have been running against the clock and found yourself with no time to fill your life with joy and happiness, you may simply need to schedule 'fun' activities into your diary. If you discovered that adopting the smiling habit had a significant impact on your lightheartedness then you can easily fit this new practice into your daily life. And many people say that the simple acts of remembering to be thankful for their lives and to count their blessings have had an amazingly positive effect on their mood. So don't wait until something or someone has gone from your life before you begin to appreciate it.

CHANGE ONE THING

RAISE YOUR HAPPINESS LEVELS TODAY BY DOING ANY ONE OF THE FOLLOWING:

- WATCH LESS TELEVISION.

- MAKE AN EFFORT TO COMMUNICATE WITH YOUR LOVED ONES.

- KEEP LAUGHING.

- BE GLAD TO BE HERE.

- PUT 100 PER CENT EFFORT INTO YOUR LIFE.

- TRUST YOUR DECISION-MAKING PROCESS.

- ASK WHEN YOU WANT SOMETHING.

- BE COMPASSIONATE AND FORGIVING.

- DANCE YOUR BLUES AWAY.

- TAKE TIME TO STAND AND STARE.

- GIVE SOMETHING TO SOMEONE.

Choosing the happiness-making strategies that work for you

Today you can review the Happiness Programme to see

precisely which of the strategies work best for you. By bringing together all the useful information that you have discovered over the previous nine days you can find out how to apply it to raise the quality of all aspects of your life. When you review the most important points and theories you can reassess their practical value. As you work through the following list of the main happiness-making strategies, ask yourself which of them could be most useful to you.

Obviously you will have found some points more relevant than others. For example, you might be a glass half-full sort of person who doesn't need to learn to choose hope over despair. On the other hand it might be hard for you to set realistic and purposeful goals. Each of us approaches life with a different mindset and what is difficult for one can be easy for another. But you can be sure that we all have our own self-doubts and personal challenges to overcome. Your day-to-day happiness depends upon an intimate knowledge of how you operate; how you think, feel and behave. And when you can recognise what you need to change and how you can do this you are well on the way to adopting the happiness habit for good.

The Happiness-Making Strategies

Get into the happiness zone by breaking the cycle of unhappiness. If your energy is stuck and you are feeling negative it's time to start expecting the best from life. Take action to break out of this negative downward spiral or you will only serve to increase your levels of misery.

Stop trying to keep everyone happy. This is an impossible task which will decrease your self-worth and self-esteem; begin to please yourself.

Become a smiler and feel the difference that this makes to just about every area of your life.

Take time to smell a rose or two. If you are a rushaholic you will never have time to be happy; it's time to slow down, wind down and simplify.

Have fun every day or you might forget what it feels like to be happy.

Know what you love to do and do more of it! This sounds so easy but it might take some planning. The more you do what you love to do the happier you will be.

Be optimistic and be ready for success. Always look for the silver lining; optimists have a happy life.

Challenge any negative beliefs. Cognitive therapy demonstrates how positive thinking can change our feelings and our behaviour.

Use positive affirmations to help you to change any negative beliefs that stand in the way of your happiness.

Expect to be happy and be ready to do what it takes.

Trust your instincts, you really do know what is good for you; take some time to listen to your inner voice.

Identify the voice of your inner critic and don't let it get to you; recognise your true worth.

Change any habits that don't work for you. You will know what these are. If you keep doing the same thing you will get the same result. If you are looking for change then do things differently.

Increase your motivation by encouraging yourself to take action; that very first small step will be enough to get you going.

Focus on what really brings you joy and satisfaction; a meaningful life is a happy life.

Recognise your own skills and talents and use them. If you are not in touch with your inner creative spark then you will find that you are on the wrong path. You will only be happy when you are doing what you are meant to do.

Know what you want. Name your goals; you cannot go for what you want if you haven't specified your outcome.

Scatter your goodwill and happy thoughts about and you will feel even more fabulous (and so will everyone around you).

Stop trying to be perfect. You will never achieve this whilst in human form. Let it go, you are good enough just the way you are.

Always choose hope rather than despair. Hope makes everything possible and opens the doorway to happiness.

Love and appreciate yourself and admire your strength of purpose; yes, you really do deserve to be happy!

Be forgiving of yourself and others. As you let go of past hurts you will bring a wonderful sense of peacefulness and calm into your life.

Believe that love is everywhere and you will find it everywhere.

Choose to be joyful. Happiness is a choice that you are free to make whenever you wish.

Stop caring about what other people think. Be yourself; stop comparing yourself with others and you will immediately feel happier.

Go for your dreams. How can you ever feel happy if you don't?

HAPPINESS TIP

CELEBRATE YOUR STAR QUALITY

WHAT IS YOUR MOST BRILLIANT FEATURE? WHERE ARE YOU AT YOUR BEST? WHERE DO YOU SHINE? ARE YOU PATIENT, HONEST, OPEN, COURAGEOUS, FUNNY, THOUGHTFUL ?

- ACCEPT ONE OF YOUR UNIQUE QUALITIES AND CONSIDER WHEN YOU LAST USED IT.

- HOW COULD YOU USE THIS ABILITY OF YOURS AGAIN?

- WHAT COULD YOU DO IN THE NEXT FEW HOURS THAT WOULD DEMONSTRATE YOUR STAR QUALITY?

Designing your own personal Happiness Action Plan

Your Happiness Action Plan is a more detailed version of the Happiness Audit that you created on Day 2. We will now take an in-depth look at all the different areas of your life (some of which will not have been revealed by the Audit).

Look at the following categories and give each of them a happiness rating using the fed-up to fabulous scale.

TOTALLY FED-UP									FABULOUS
1	2	3	4	5	6	7	8	9	10

Consider where you are right now in each of these areas of your life and then think about where you would like to be.

Category	Happiness rating	Where I am	Where I would like to be
Self-image	…………..	………………..	……………..
Health and Fitness	…………..	………………..	……………..

Money	....	....	....
Love	....	....	....
Friends	....	....	....
Family	....	....	....
Emotional Wellbeing	....	....	....
Community	....	....	....
Career	....	....	....
Leisure	....	....	....
Other	....	....	....

Take some time over this and record your details in your journal. The object of this exercise is to clarify exactly what you need to do to increase your happiness levels in each area of your life. You might just need a change of attitude to increase your happiness rating or you might need to get down to making some lifestyle changes.

Refer back to the list of happiness-making strategies starting on page 222. Which of these could you use to increase your happiness levels? Here are a few examples of how to translate your personal information into an action plan that will lift your spirits.

Example: I score a happiness rating of 3 for the Self-Image category. I describe myself as having a poor body image and feeling very negative. I would like to be fitter and toned and more upbeat. When I refer to the list of strategies I decide that I need to act in more than one way if I want to feel happier. I need to challenge my negative self-beliefs and I must set some realistic health and fitness goals.

Example: I score 2 for happiness in the Community section. I have just moved to a new area away from my friends and am feeling a bit lost. I want to get to know some people. I decide to adopt the smiling habit (I have been acting grumpily) and I will also join the local tennis club (I enjoy playing and I will meet some new people).

Example: I score 1 for Money. I am fed-up with being broke and I would love to be able to buy a new car. Before I look at the list I know what I have to do; I must change my spending habits. I need to plug those money drains by stopping myself buying new clothes every week. I plan to open a savings account and to put away a regular amount of my salary cheque and then I will be able to afford a car in eight months.

Example: I score 2 for Love. I keep having useless relationships with unsuitable guys. I want to have a committed relationship with someone who loves me. I decide to stop looking for a new man and to spend time on my own for a while. I need to recognise my skills and talents and get using them and then I would feel happier in myself. I am in a job that doesn't stretch me so I plan to take control of my future by making a new career move (I scored 2 for career as well). I am feeling better about myself already! I also need to adopt a more optimistic 'can-do' approach; pessimism is bringing me down.

Example: I score 4 for Family. I have had a disagreement with my sister-in-law and now my brother has stopped talking to me as well. I need to be more forgiving so that we can all make up again. A minor issue blew up out of all proportion and someone needs to make amends and I think I can do that. It would be great if we can all meet up at family gatherings the way we used to. I could also start to scatter some goodwill to the other people in my life; I have been complaining a lot lately.

ACTIVITY: I AM SURE

SOMETIMES THINGS FEEL VERY UNCERTAIN AND ON SUCH A DAY IT CAN BE DIFFICULT TO FIND THE COURAGE AND CONVICTION WE NEED TO MAINTAIN OUR GOOD SPIRITS. BUT THERE ARE SOME THINGS OF WHICH YOU CAN BE SURE AND THESE CAN GIVE YOU A BOOST OF CONFIDENCE WHEN YOU MOST NEED IT.

LIST SIX THINGS THAT YOU ARE SURE THAT YOU CAN DO WELL.

EXAMPLE:

I AM SURE THAT I AM A GOOD FRIEND.
I AM SURE THAT I CAN GROW DELICIOUS VEGETABLES.
I AM SURE THAT I CAN COOK A GREAT MEAL.
I AM SURE THAT I AM A GOOD MUM.
I AM SURE THAT I AM A DETERMINED PERSON.
I AM SURE THAT I KNOW HOW TO USE A COMPUTER.

LET THIS ACTIVITY REMIND YOU OF YOUR TALENTS AND

Applying your Happiness Action Plan

When we are feeling less than our best we are inclined to
lose confidence in ourselves and it can seem an
overwhelming task to locate exactly what is going wrong and
why. Happily, the coaching model creates a constructive
framework, which can always help us to get clear about what
we want (however muddled we might be feeling). Rather
than dwelling on 'problems' it takes a solution-based
approach. This is a positive way forward that stops the
endless analysing and conceptualising and worrying that can
create even more unhappiness and doubt when we are
already feeling down. Sometimes clients have been thinking
so hard about why they are fed-up that they have convinced
themselves that their situation is their fault in some way; this
attitude can never lead to a positive solution.

Denise's story

Denise, 46, had emailed me to ask if I thought that coaching
could help her. She said that she felt in a daze most of the time
as if she was running on autopilot and that she had lost her
zest and joy for life. I wrote back saying that I thought that a
few sessions could certainly help her and then I didn't hear
from her again for some months. Next time she wrote to book
some coaching appointments and we got down to work.

Denise was married with older children who were coming
to the end of their school life and she worked as a
receptionist at an orthodontic surgery near her home. She
said that she couldn't understand what was happening to her

but that everything about her life was feeling difficult and that she was unhappy most of the time. Derek, her husband, was very supportive but was at a loss to know what to do.

I gave Denise the task of creating her own Happiness Action Plan, using exactly the same format as you have used on page 226. By breaking up the life categories in this way Denise was able to focus on exactly what was going on in her life. Her happiness ratings were low for self-image; health and fitness; emotional wellbeing and leisure. She was financially secure and felt well supported by her family and friends and the local community.

We took each of her low rating items separately, looking at where she was and where she wanted to be, and then we worked together to find a solution. For self-image she scored 1 and described herself as overweight and feeling middle aged and less sexually attractive. She wanted to lose what she described as her 'middle-aged spread' so that she could get into some new and fashionable clothes. For health and fitness she scored 3 and said that she was totally unfit and that she felt particularly unwell when she was menstruating. She thought that she might be moving into the menopause and this frightened her because her own mother had a very hard time dealing with this and she was worried that she might too. Denise didn't really want to talk about how she might resolve this; she said 'I would rather not think about the menopause'. For emotional wellbeing she scored 4 and described her feelings as being inconsistent; sometimes she would be fine and then suddenly for no apparent reason she would feel anxious. Of course she wanted to get her emotions back on an even keel. In the leisure category she scored 3 because she was always too tired to make any plans; she said that she would love to get out more and that Derek was always suggesting places to go but that she just couldn't get her motivation together.

As we talked more about her concerns Denise began to find it easier to accept that she was facing great changes in her life. She admitted that she was dreading her children leaving home and also dreading the menopause.

Her Happiness Action Plan revolved around using some simple happiness-making strategies to lift her negativity. She worked on her attitude and her optimism and as she did so she became more hopeful of the future. On another level she realised that she needed some support to deal with the physical changes that she was going through. She set up an appointment with her doctor and also got in touch with the Women's Nutritional Advisory Service through the internet. Once she had looked at all her options she chose to follow a plan suggested by the WNAS, which had considered her diet, supplementary nutritional needs and her exercise levels.

At this point our coaching ended but she was already following a planned approach to relieving her health and fitness issues. Three months later she dropped me an email to say that she was back on track and feeling her old self with bags of energy (and she had lost some weight).

When you are ready to create an action plan to increase your happiness levels you will feel that you are regaining control of your life and this in itself will make you feel much happier. If you are feeling unhappy and out of control just get going on your Happiness Action Plan: look at the categories and find out where you need to make changes, consider what you need to do and then do it!

CHANGE ONE THING

BY MAKING WAY FOR THE NEW

IF YOU WANT TO BRING MORE OF ANYTHING INTO YOUR LIFE THEN YOU NEED TO LET GO OF SOMETHING FIRST. BY LETTING GO OF WHAT DOESN'T WORK YOU MAKE WAY TO RECEIVE MORE OF WHAT YOU WANT. DON'T LET OLD STUFF DRAG YOU DOWN.

- LET GO OF BORING HABITS AND OPEN UP TO EXCITING NEW EXPERIENCES.

- LET GO OF OLD COMPLAINTS AND GRUDGES AND YOU WILL FEEL MORE AT EASE WITH LIFE.

- LET GO OF THE THOUGHTS THAT MAKE YOU UNHAPPY; FOCUS ON HAPPINESS.

- LET GO OF YOUR CLUTTER; YOU WILL HAVE MORE PHYSICAL SPACE AND YOU WILL ALSO FEEL PSYCHOLOGICALLY LIGHTER.

- LET GO OF YOUR FEARS AND TRUST THAT THE UNIVERSE WILL BRING YOU ALL THAT YOU NEED.

Refresh yourself

When we are happy our energy is balanced and harmonious and we feel relaxed and chilled! Over the years I have noticed that the clients who benefit most from coaching are those who incorporate some 'time outs' into their lives.

Although it can sometimes feel that we *must do more* to achieve whatever we are after this is not always the case; we actually find it easier to make changes when we are relaxed and at ease.

If you are feeling overwhelmed then it is vitally important that you take some time out of your schedule to just 'be'. And if you feel that you really haven't got any spare moments, then think again. How can you ever be happy if you don't have time for yourself? If happiness is your priority then prioritise it! Find the time to be happy.

From a holistic standpoint we exist at a number of interconnected levels: our mind, body, spirit and emotions react together to create the quality of our experiences. When we are feeling calm and centred we are linking with our spiritual aspect and this helps to connect us with the rest of the universe. We have all had those 'wow' moments when we tap into a deep level of appreciation for life and it is that connection that we are talking about here. Perhaps you saw an amazing view or heard a wonderful piece of music or enjoyed a great piece of art or watched a child being born . . . There are so many breathtaking experiences on offer when we open up to our spiritual energy and allow ourselves to see the wonder that surrounds us.

The Refresh and Renew sessions at the end of each chapter have been specifically designed to give you space to unwind each day. When we are stretched and stressed we can never feel truly contented, so these meditations and visualisations are important for your wellbeing and will allow you to open your heart to happiness. Make sure that you fit some of these sessions into your Happiness Action Plan and they will help to smooth away your worries and bring joy into your life.

REFRESH AND RENEW

INVOCATION

To invoke means to 'call in' or 'call upon' and you can use the power of invocation to visualise and affirm any quality that you wish for yourself.

So just sit or lie down, close your eyes and follow your breathing until you feel relaxed and centred.

- When you are feeling focused, say to yourself silently but firmly, *I now call forth the quality of happiness.*

- Feel the energy of happiness filling your mind. You are full of happy thoughts.

- Now feel happiness infuse your emotions. You are full of happy feelings.

- Let happy energy enter your every cell and feel your whole body vibrating with positivity and joy.

- Stay with these uplifting feelings for as long as you wish.

Travel along the happiness highway

I love reading self-help books (as well as writing them) because they remind me of what I am most inclined to forget: that I need to keep working on myself! I may know 1001 ways to feel happy but I don't always remember to use them! And I expect that you are the same. You might have worked hard to break a negative thought pattern or a bad habit and then just found yourself effortlessly slipping back into your old ways again. If this sounds like you then don't be disheartened; we are all inclined to take a step backwards sometimes. At this crucial point, when you might start to criticise your strength of will, lack of courage, self-doubt, etc., just become aware of what you are doing and stop; know that this path will not make you happy. The happiness highway is the route that always supports and empowers you; it is positively affirming, optimistic and realistic. Try the techniques and strategies in this book and find the ones that have the most positive effect on you. And when you know what they are *keep using them!*

Clients are often surprised when I tell them that I have positive affirmations stuck up in my house. They are even more surprised when I reveal that I can be self-doubting at times. But although I can be grumpy and self-critical and negative I won't stay there for long because it makes me feel bad! Why should I be unhappy when I could be happy? And why should you?

Isn't it fabulous to know that we can learn to be optimistic? And as the new positive psychology (science of happiness) has demonstrated: we can increase our happiness levels whenever we choose. We know that the research shows that happiness can create success and we can confirm the truth of this in our own everyday experience. The happier we are the more positive and hopeful we feel, and our increased enthusiasm and motivation attracts new people and fresh opportunities into our life.

Your search for happiness is a journey rather than a goal and it's worth reminding yourself of this on a daily basis. You are travelling along a path that will sometimes be bumpy and at other times will be smooth but if you tread lightly, with happiness in your heart, you will always feel glad to be alive.

I had such a great time writing this book, and all the while it was a constant reminder to me that I could choose to be happy whenever I wished. I do hope that you have enjoyed reading it and that it has helped you to see how easy it is for you to change your mood from fed-up to fabulous. If you would like to get in touch with me or find out more about my life-coaching services just go to www.weekendlifecoach.com or email me at lyndafield@weekendlifecoach.com

I look forward to hearing from you.

With all my best wishes

Lynda

References and
Inspirational Books

Over the years I have gathered many wonderful quotes
from a variety of sources, including books, television and
radio broadcasts, magazine articles and newspaper features.
I would particularly like to acknowledge my use of the
following collections of quotations: *The Columbia
Dictionary of Quotations,* compiled by Robert Andrews
(New York: Columbia University Press, 1993); *Bartlett's
Familiar Quotations,* Sixteenth Edition, edited by Justin
Kaplan (Boston: Little, Brown and Company, 1992;
www.wisdomquotes.com; www.quotationspage.com;
www.bartleby.com; www.quotedb.com and
www.dict.die.net

Beck, Aaron T, *Cognitive Therapy for Challenging
Problems*, Guilford Press, 2005

Christie, Agatha, *An Autobiography,* HarperCollins, 2001

Covey, Steven, *The Seven Habits of Highly Effective People,*
Simon & Schuster UK Ltd, 1999

Csikszentmihalyi, Mihaly, *Flow: The Classic Work on How to
Achieve Happiness*, Rider, 2002

HH Dalai Lama and Cutler, Howard C, *The Art of Happiness*,
Hodder & Stoughton, 1999

Edmonds, Noel, *Positively Happy*, Vermilion, 2006

Field, Lynda, *Be Yourself*, Vermilion, 2003

— *Weekend Life Coach*, Vermilion, 2004

— *Instant Life Coach*, Vermilion, 2005

— *Weekend Confidence Coach*, Vermilion, 2006

Goleman, Daniel, *Emotional Intelligence,* Bloomsbury, 1996

Greenberger, Dennis and Padesky, Christine A, *Mind Over Mood*, Guilford Press, 1995

Hanh, Thich Nhat, *The Miracle of Mindfulness*, Rider, 1991

— *Peace is Every Step*, Rider, 1995

Hay, Louise, *You Can Heal Your Life*, Eden Grove Editions, 1988

Hoggard, Liz, *How to be Happy*, BBC Books, 2005

Holden, Barbara Warren, *Diamonds, Pearls and Stones,* Health Communications, 2004

Holden, Robert, *The Happiness Project,* www.happiness.co.uk

Honoré, Carl, *In Praise of Slow*, Orion, 2005

Kabat-Zinn, Jon, *Mindfulness Meditation for Everyday Life*, Piatkus, 1994

— *Coming to Our Senses*, Piatkus, 2005

Kelly, Bob, *Worth Repeating,* Kregel Academic & Professional, 2003

MacDonald, Lucy, *Learn to Be an Optimist*, Duncan Baird Publishers, 2004

Mueller, F. Max (trans.), *The Wisdom of The Buddha: The Unabridged Dhammapada*, Dover Publications Inc, 2000

Nietzsche, Friedrich, *Thus Spoke Zarathusa,* translated by Walter Kaufmann, Penguin, 1978

Niven, David, *The 100 Simple Secrets of Happy People*, Capstone Publishing Ltd, 2005

Pegg, Mike, *The Art of Encouragement*, Enhance, 1995

Pradervand, Pierre, *The Gentle Art of Blessing*, Cygnus Books, 2004

Roman, Sanaya, *Living with Joy*, H. J. Kramer Inc, 1986

Ruiz, Don Miguel, *The Four Agreements*, Amber-Allen Publishing, 1997

Schaef, Anne Wilson, *Meditations for Women Who Do Too Much*, HarperCollins, 1996

Seligman, Martin, *Authentic Happiness*, Nicholas Brealey Publishing Ltd, 2003

Shapiro, Stephen, *Goal Free Living*, John Wiley & Sons Inc, 2006

Steinem, Gloria, *Revolution from Within*, Little, Brown & Company, 1992

Tagore, Rabindranath, *Stray Birds*, Kessinger Publishing Co, 2004

Vilord, Thomas, *1001 Motivational Quotes for Success,* Garden State Publishing, 2004

Index